DAY TRADING FOR BEGINNERS:

© Copyright 2019 - All rights reserved.

The content contained within this book may not be reproduced, duplicated or transmitted without direct written permission from the author or the publisher.

Under no circumstances will any blame or legal responsibility be held against the publisher, or author, for any damages, reparation, or monetary loss due to the information contained within this book. Either directly or indirectly.

Legal Notice:

This book is copyright protected. This book is only for personal use. You cannot amend, distribute, sell, use, quote or paraphrase any part, or the content within this book, without the consent of the author or publisher.

Disclaimer Notice:

Please note the information contained within this document is for educational and entertainment purposes only. All effort has been executed to present accurate, up to date, and reliable, complete information. No warranties of any kind are declared or implied. Readers acknowledge that the author is not engaging in the rendering of legal, financial, medical or professional advice. The content within this book has been derived from various sources. Please consult a licensed professional before attempting any techniques outlined in this book.

By reading this document, the reader agrees that under no circumstances is the author responsible for any losses, direct or indirect, which are incurred as a result of the use of information contained within this document, including, but not limited to, — errors, omissions, or inaccuracies.

Description

Introduction

Chapter 1 What is day trading?

Chapter 2 Dos and Don'ts of Day Trading

Chapter 3 Personalizing Your Day Trading Plans

Chapter 4 Finding and Picking Stocks and Trading Strategies

Chapter 5 Demand and Supply and Market Types

Chapter 6 Developing Your Day Trading Strategy

Chapter 7 Trading *Psychology*

Chapter 8 Support or Resistance Trading

Chapter 9 Fibonacci Trading Strategy

Chapter 10 Finding Entry and Exit Points

Chapter 11 Portfolio Diversification

Chapter 12 Managing Risk in Trading and the Role of Journaling

Chapter 13 Tips and Tricks to Make Your Life Easier when Using the MT4 Platform

Conclusion

Description

With the millions of people who exchange dollars in the online trading market, any investor should understand that there is a huge potential worth taking advantage of in trading. One important question that new traders should ask themselves is whether trading the right activity for them.

Before you engage in trading, you should have the right reasons why you need to trade. In this case, it could be that you want to grow your capital and open a thriving business. Also, you might be willing to trade for the benefit of gaining experience out of it. Depending on the reasons that you have in mind, they should motivate you in trading. This means that you will end up trading without any regrets if things fail to work out as planned.

You will need a sober mind to succeed in day trading. Unfortunately, there are common mental errors which could affect how well you perform in your trading activity. For instance, if you lack confidence in your plan, how do you expect to stick to it? You have to believe that your plan will lead you to make profits that you anticipate. This mentality will develop a positive attitude about the whole trading activity. Therefore, you will have all the reasons to be disciplined and stick to your plans no matter the circumstances.

Most importantly, you should always remember that there is a lot to learn from day trading. It doesn't matter whether you succeed or fail in day trading; once you begin trading, there are important real-life lessons that you can take home. You will be in a better position to make more informed decisions.

This book gives a comprehensive guide on the following:

- What is day trading?
- Dos and Don'ts of Day Trading
- Personalizing Your Day Trading Plans
- Finding and Picking Stocks and Trading Strategies
- Demand and Supply and Market Types
- Developing Your Day Trading Strategy
- Trading Psychology
- Support or Resistance Trading
- Fibonacci Trading Strategy
- Finding Entry and Exit Points

- Portfolio Diversification
- Managing Risk in Trading ... AND MORE!!!

Introduction

While there will obviously be some differences when day trading in different markets, there are always going to be a number of steps that are the same. First, you will need to locate an underling asset that you are interested in trading based on your research which should be based on either fundamental or technical analysis. Second, you will need to decide if it aligns with your personal trading plan as just because a trade is potential profitable doesn't mean it is going to be the right choice for you, right now. From there, assuming you are still interested in making the trade, you can then take a position that you believe will soon be profitable based on the current state of the market. Finally, you will do the same thing around 100 times a day.

Pros and cons of day trading

While the above description might make it sound as though day trade is relatively straightforward, the fact of the matter is that it is an extremely complex process requiring the successful use of a variety of tools and skills that not everyone will be able to follow through on reliably. As such, this list of pros and cons should make it easier for you to determine if this type of trading is one that you are interested pursuing in the long-term in search of your ultimate financial goals.

Pros: The biggest pro when it comes to day trading is the potential for gain when everything goes according to plan. The average successful day trader tends to buy a large number of shares at a time to ensure that they stand to make a serious profit from even an extremely small amount of movement. Additionally, they have the potential to work for themselves, only trading when they feel the urge or when the market is in a place that is too good to pass up.

Another major benefit to day trading for certain types of traders is the amount of excitement they can expect to see on a daily basis. As they only ever trade in the absolute shortest timeframes, the average day trader sees far more action than most other types of traders would in the same amount of time. What's more, day trading provides those who are up to the challenge with the opportunity to face off with many of the best traders in the world, dozens, if not hundreds of times each day. If you are the sort of thrill seeker who is sure to appreciate a good spike of adrenaline then day trading might be for you.

Another benefit to day trading is that you can teach yourself as easily as you can pay someone else to teach you what to do, making it one of the few ways you can get a job in the financial sector with a formal education. As long as you are willing and able to put in the time and dedicated enough to see it through to the end, then there is no reason you can't acquire the skills you need on your own and then hone them through countless hours of practice.

Cons: The biggest downside to day trading has to do with the wide variety of costs associated with being able to do so successfully. As they are dealing with very small amounts of movement, day traders need a sizeable amount of trading capital just to get off the ground. An amount of around $20,000 should be enough to let you get started in a truly productive fashion. Beyond that, the number of daily trades being made means that the costs paid in commission are going to be far higher than with most other types of trading.

Not only that but due to the high number of shares that come along with the average trade in this field, the potential for loss if a trade turns against you can be quite significant as well. In fact, statistically speaking, day trading is the most difficult type of securities trading to make a profit from in any sort of reliable fashion. In fact, a majority of new day traders experience mostly losses for at least the first month, and only about 30 percent move on from that state to be able to reliably turn a profit.

What's more, the monetary issues aren't the only barriers to entry either, and one of the biggest is the fact that the average amateur day trader is generally competing against professional organizations with a cadre of traders at their disposal and pockets that are extremely deep. As such, if you want to hope to chance of entering the market successfully then you will need to be prepared for what you are up against. Finally, many brokerages will simply not let you day trade in any way shape or form until you have already proven that you are capable of trading in a competent fashion on a more manageable scale to start.

In addition to these issues, the fact that the average day trader is self-employed means that it will simply not be the right choice for those who don't have the internal fortitude to put in the required work without having a boss standing over your shoulder ensuring that they are doing all that is needed for them to be successful. What's more, the average day trader has to fend for themselves when it comes to things like health insurance, a steady retirement plan or even a steady paycheck.

Chapter 1 What is day trading?

The stock market is a vast place and there are millions of trades that take place all over the world, within a single day. There are both buyers and sellers in the market and they will all have the same motive in mind; to increase their wealth potential.

Of all these trades, not everything will be of the same nature. Some will be long-term investments and some short. Long-term investments refer to those that are held for a long period of time. They are preferred by those who are not in a hurry to make money. Short-term investments on the other hand are those that are liquidated within a short period of time. They are not meant to be held for a long time, as the owners will be interested in disposing them off early.

Short-term investments can be of many types based on the time that they are held. Some can be held for a month, some for a week and some will be disposed off on the same day. This book will focus on the last option.

Better known as Intraday trading, day trading is one of the most preferred ways to trade in the stock market. Preferred mostly by those willing to part with their investment within a single day and realize a profit, or loss, from.

Intraday traders are interested in realizing a profit by capitalizing on the difference in the rates of these securities as opposed to long-term investors who will be in it for the Dividends.

Intraday trading has the capacity to help you attain a big leverage, as the rate of return on your investments can be quite high. However, it can also go the other way and cause you to lose out on a lot of money owing to poor investments. It is up to you to make the right choices and invest your money wisely.

Chapter 2 Dos and Don'ts of Day Trading

Dos of day trading

Risk capital

You have to understand that the stock market is a very volatile place and anything can happen within a matter of a few seconds. You have to be prepared for anything that it throws at you. In order to prepare for it, you have to make use of risk capital. Risk capital refers to money that you are willing to risk. You have to convince yourself that even if you lose the money that you have invested then it will not be a big deal for you. For that, you have to make use of your own money and not borrow from anyone, as you will start feeling guilty about investing it. Decide on a set number and invest it.

Research

You have to conduct a thorough research on the market before investing in it. Don't think you will learn as you go. That is only possible if you at least know the basics. You have to remain interested in gathering information that is crucial for your investments and it will only come about if you put in some hard work towards it. Nobody is asking you to stay up and go through thick texts books. All you have to do is go through books and websites and gather enough information to help you get started on the right foot.

Diversification

You have to stress on diversification in your portfolio. You don't want all the money to go into the same place. Think of it as a way to increase your stock's potential. You have to choose different sectors and diverse stocks to invest in. you should also choose one of the different types of investments as they all contribute towards attaining a different result. Diversification is mostly seen, as a tool to cut down on risk and it is best that you not invest any more than 5% in any one of the securities.

Stop loss

You have to understand the importance of a stop loss mechanism. A stop loss technique is used to safeguard an investment. Now say for example you invest $100 and buy shares priced at $5 each. You have to place a stop loss at around $4 in order to stop it from going down any further. Now you will wonder as to why you have to place the stop loss and undergo one, well, by doing so, you will actually be saving your money to a large extent. You won't have to worry about the value slipping further down and can carry on with your trade.

Take a loss

It is fine to take a loss from time to time. Don't think of it as a big hurdle. You will have the chance the convert the loss into a profit. You have to remain confident and invested. You can take a loss on a bad investment that was anyway not going your way. You can also take a loss on an investment that you think is a long hold and will not work for you in the short term. Taking a few losses is the only way in which you can learn to trade well in the market.

These form the different dos of the stock market that will help you with your intraday trades.

Don'ts of day trading

No planning

Do not make the mistake of going about investing in the market without a plan in tow. You have to plan out the different things that you will do in the market and go about it the right way. This plan should include how much you will invest in the market, where you will invest, how you will go about it etc. No planning will translate to getting lost in the stock market, which is not a good sign for any investor.

Over rely on broker

You must never over rely on a broker. You have to make your own decisions and know what to do and when. The broker will not know whether an investment is good for you. He will only be bothered about his profits. If he is suggesting something, then you should do your own research before investing in the stock. The same extends to emails that you might receive through certain sources. These emails are spams and meant to dupe you. So, don't make the mistake of trusting everything that you read.

Message boards

You have to not care about message boards. These will be available on the Internet and are mostly meant to help people gather information. But there will be pumpers and bashers present there. Pumpers will force people to buy a stock just to increase its value and bashers will force people to sell all their stocks just because they want the value to go down. Both these types are risky, as they will abandon the investors just as soon as their motive is fulfilled. So you have to be quite carful with it.

Calculate wrong

Some people make the mistake of calculating wrong. They will not be adept at math and will end up with wrong figures. This is a potential danger to all those looking to increase their wealth potential. If you are not god at calculating, then download n app that will do it for you or carry a calculator around to do the correct calculations. The motive is to make the right calculations and increase your wealth potential.

Copy strategies

Do not make the mistake of copying someone else's strategies. You have to come up with something that is your own and not borrowed from someone else. If you end up borrowing, then you will not be able to attain the desired results. You have to sit with your broker and come up with a custom strategy that you can employ and win big.

These form the different don'ts of the stock market that will help you keep troubles at bay.

Chapter 3 Personalizing Your Day Trading Plans

While we have discussed some of the trading strategies that I found to work best for me, there's still a chance that they may not be the best ones for you, though they're good places to start. As you become more experienced with day trading, you'll probably have to tweak these strategies or revamp them, depending on your day trading results.

Regardless, the best day trading plans are those that are most suited to your personality and your goals. In this chapter, let's take a look at some of the important things you'll need to consider when personalizing your day trading strategies or plans.

Your Strengths and Weaknesses

To optimize your day trading plans' chances of helping you accomplish your goals, it must be one that you can actually use. By this, I mean your day trading strategy should be one that's commensurate to your current level of trading or investing experience. That's why if you remember, I encouraged you to practice on your chosen trading platform's simulator first before day trading for real.

Remember that day trading is a very fast-paced activity and as such, it requires very quick decision making. And you can only make wise and quick trading decisions if you have enough experience and skill.

If you're not the type of person who can easily make quick decisions under pressure, then go for simpler day trading plans like moving averages, which allow longer decision-making periods and provide clearer entry and exit points. If you're very comfortable with making such decisions and have already gained enough experience and skills through practice, you can use the more advanced strategies.

Your Non-Trading, Personal Circumstances

Creating a generally successful trading plan, you'll also need to factor things outside of day trading that may affect your ability to execute such plans effectively. These may be personal circumstances or situations such as lack of fast internet connection, working a day job, or going through personal challenges. I'm not saying that you should only adopt strategies or plans that will not be affected by such circumstances. I'm just saying that you must take into consideration these things so that you can anticipate challenges they may face and proactively develop solutions to address them, should they arise.

Your Risk Appetite

Your maximum position size and maximum trading amount, both of which are crucial components of any day trading plan, must not be above and beyond your personal risk appetite or tolerance. If you take positions or trade amounts that are greater than what you're comfortable risking, your chances of trading based on strong emotions like fear or anxiety will be very, very high. It's because your trading more than what you feel you're capable of losing without any major impact on your personal finances.

So, how do you estimate your personal risk tolerance or appetite? One way is to get five percent of your maximum trading capital or equity and make this your single position-taking limit if you have no clear idea of your risk appetite just yet.

Another way to determine your risk appetite is to determine how much time can you really devote to day trading on a daily basis. The less time you can devote to day trading daily, the higher your risk appetite should be because less time means fewer opportunities to monitor and time your day trades optimally.

Another way to determine risk appetite is to ask yourself: How much money can I lose comfortably? Not that you're day trading to make money but the truth is, you'll expose yourself to risk of losing trades, too. Even the best veteran day traders still have losing trades, but the difference is that their total day trading profits are much greater than their day trading losses.

Chapter 4 Finding and Picking Stocks and Trading Strategies

In this chapter, we get down to the actual work of day trading. We will cover how to read the market by discussing the types of charts used by day traders and how to read them. We'll also discuss strategies for picking stocks and what to look for in stocks for day trading. Finally, we'll cover the most common trading strategies and how to execute them.

Reading the Market

We've already discussed charts and charting software in passing. Now you need to know how to read the charts your software or your broker provide to you. There's three basic types of charts you're likely to look at when you're reading the market: line charts, bar charts, and "candlestick" charts.

Line Charts: line charts are the simplest type of chart you are likely to use while day trading. A line chart tracks only the closing prices for your selected time interval and will display as a jagged line from left to right. This is the type of chart you are probably most familiar with outside of the world of trading, and it provides the least information of the common chart types. However, many traders still use line charts for certain trading strategies. Since a line chart is less cluttered, it can make inflection points in the market more obvious to the eye and can be useful for drawing lines to identify ranges or trends.

Bar Charts: bar charts, also known as OHLC bar charts or HLC bar charts, include information on the open (O), high (H), low (L), and close (C) price of an asset over a given time interval. The chart will appear as a series of horizontal lines following the same sort of jagged line you would see in a simple line chart, with a small line jutting from each side at the open and close. There's a lot of information in these charts, so it may take quite a bit of practice to get used to reading them.

Open: the open on a bar chart is the opening price for the time interval and shows on the chart as a small line sticking out of the left side of the bar.

High: the high price during the interval is indicated by the top of the bar.

Low: the low price for the interval is indicated by the bottom the bar.

Close: the closing price for the interval shows as a small line sticking out of the right side of the bar.

Direction: you can tell the direction of the market during the interval by comparing the positions of the opening and closing prices for the interval. If the open is higher, the market is moving down. If the close is higher, the market is moving up.

Candlestick Charts: candlestick charts contain the same information as bar charts but presented in a different fashion that many traders find easier to read. At a glance, the candlestick chart will look similar to a bar chart, but more colorful. Each time interval will display as a colored bar (the "body" of the candle), red or green, with a line (the "tail") extending some distance above and below the body of the candlestick. Here's how the information is represented:

High: the high price for the interval is indicated by the top of the tail above the candle.

Low: the low price for the interval is indicated by the bottom of the tail below the candle.

Open: the opening price for the interval is indicated by the bottom of the body of the candle.

Close: the closing price for the interval is indicated by the top of the body of the candle.

Direction: the direction of the market is indicated by the color of the body of the candle - red if the market is moving down, green if the market is moving up.

Chart Parameters: when generating a chart, you will need to pick the interval that will be represented by each point in your chart. The interval could be based on time, "tick", volume, or price range.

A chart generated by time is the most intuitive, and will generate a new bar, candle, or point based purely on the passage of time - even if very few or even no transactions occurred during the interval. This is the most useful way to generate a chart if you are looking to see how a stock or asset performs in real time.

A chart generated by "tick" uses an interval based on a set number of transactions. For example, if you generate a 200-tick chart, the graph will produce a new point every time 200 transactions occur. This can be useful for comparing trends between stocks with different levels of activity.

A chart generated by volume will generate intervals based on a set number of shares exchanged.

You will also need to define the scope of the chart. Depending on your strategy, you may want to look at a chart for the entire trading day, or a chart that covers the last minute.

Trend lines: most trading software allows you to draw your own trend lines on charts or will have options for displaying trends such as the simple moving average automatically. While you can get a lot of information just from your chart without trends, most of the decisions you will make in executing your trading strategy will come from looking at trend lines.

Picking Stocks

Now that you know the basics of reading the market and looking for trends, you're ready to learn about how to pick stocks for day trading. The type of stock you will be looking for depends on a lot of different factors, and you may be looking for different types of stocks to fit different trading plans and different trading strategies. We'll cover this topic in three parts: (1) things you should look for every stock you plan to trade while day trading; (2) some broad-based picking strategies for different trading plans; and (3) the distinct characteristics of stocks that are suitable for specific day-trading strategies.

(1) Things to Look for in Every Stock You Plan to Day-Trade: while what you're looking for will be different depending on what strategy you're planning to execute, there are a couple things you should always be looking for when picking stocks.

The first is volume: you should always look for stocks that have a high level of daily activity. If you buy into a stock with insufficient volume, you can easily find yourself stuck - the asset price won't move enough for you to take profit and you'll lose out on other trading opportunities until you can move out of your position. Typically, you should be looking for a stock that has an average daily volume of at least 1 million shares.

The second is volatility: you are looking for stocks that will move enough in a typical day for you to make a profitable trade. Set your stock filter to look for stocks with an average day range above 5% over the last 50 days. It's important to remember that volatility is not necessarily the massive up or down swings that can follow breaking news - it can also be the regular and constant turbulence that exists in all exchange traded markets.

(2) Broad Strategies for Picking Stocks: you need a broad strategy for picking stocks beyond simply looking for the desirable characteristics discussed in this chapter. How you go about researching and picking stocks depends on how much time you have available to trade and how much research you are willing to do.

If you don't have much time to trade, you may wish to specialize. That is, pick one or two stocks, or a single industry sector (such as healthcare), and only trade in those stocks or that sector. This lets you become an expert in those stocks: you know how they usually behave, where the opportunities will be, and what news events will cause swings and how. This means that you don't have to spend a lot of time sifting through charts or learning the basic facts about new companies - you already know what's likely to happen. A popular way to execute this strategy is to target an ETF, such as the S&P 500 SPDR (Ticker symbol SPY). Specializing like this works well with a range-trading or "trade the news" strategy.

If you're looking for a little bit more flexibility, you might choose to pick a set of stocks to trade each week. Each weekend, run a stock screener to identify a set of 2-4 stocks that have good volume and volatility for your trading strategy. After you have picked your stocks for the week, trade those stocks, and only those stocks following your trading plan. If you've achieved good results, you could choose to remain on the same set of securities for multiple weeks in a row. This strategy is suitable for a trader who has a little more time to dedicate to day trading but isn't prepared to trade full time.

If you're looking to pursue a full-time career as a day trader, you might choose to run a stock screener every single day. This is probably what you want to be doing if you are pursuing a momentum strategy - as you will be trying to identify stocks that have a strong current trend, instead of trying to capitalize on small movements caused by underlying volatility. Obviously, this strategy is very time consuming, and may require additional tools to execute effectively.

(3) Distinct Characteristics Suitable for Specific Strategies: depending on your strategy, you may be looking for more specific factors than simple volume and volatility.

If you are looking to trade on a momentum strategy, you should look at stocks that are close to 52-week highs and lows. Stocks that have reached extreme price points are more likely to be volatile or to be close to an inflection point that can afford a big trading opportunity.

You may also want to keep an eye out for stocks that have a gap against the trend. That is, if you look at your chart of the stock's current price, you'll see that there is a space (a "gap") between the price and the trend-line. This is a good way to identify stocks that have been overbought or oversold, or where the stock price has failed to adjust to breaking news. The moment when the gap closes is the moment when you have an opportunity to make a profitable trade.

Finally, you can set up a scanner to identify specific situations where there is an opportunity to trade based on a specific pattern in the market. One example of this is a method commonly referred to as "sniper" trading, which was originally implemented on the FOREX market.

An Overview of Common Day Trading Strategies

By sticking to your strategy, you maintain a stable level of risk and can reliably make your expected earnings goals. Here's a quick overview of some of the most common strategies for setting entry points and price targets.

Scalping: Scalping is one of the most common strategies for day trading, and with good reason - it's incredibly simple. When you are using a scalping strategy, your target price is essentially whatever price is high enough to make your trade profitable over commission. It's as easy as that: pick your asset, pick your entry point, and sell as soon as it's profitable for you. As always, make sure you have set a stop-loss if you have misjudged the buy and bought into a downward trend.

Fading: In many ways, a fading strategy is the opposite of scalping. When you are scalping, you are looking to profit on an upward trend - while fading, you are looking to profit on a downward trend. Scalping is absurdly simple, while fading requires a fairly high degree of sophistication to be really successful. Here's a basic overview: a trader who is using a fade strategy looks for a stock that has risen very quickly. Having identified a potential trade, the trader shorts the stock. The price target is a predicted low inflection point where buyers begin to step in after profit-takers exit.

This probably seems counter intuitive to a trader starting out, since it requires you to bet a stock that has been on an upward tear is going to fall in the same day. So, here's a quick explanation of the reasoning behind a fade strategy: (1) a stock that has risen very quickly is probably overbought - the price has been driven higher than demand can justify; (2) early buyers are probably ready to start profit taking - you can expect that traders who bought into the trend early are ready to unload stock, dropping the price; and (3) existing buyers may be scared out of purchasing at the current, inflated price - creating an opportunity to short the stock at a point below the peak, but above where the upward trend started.

Fading is a risky strategy, since it requires you to identify a very specific situation - but, as always, higher risk can yield higher rewards than a low-risk strategy like scalping. You may wish to consider a fading strategy after you have gotten comfortable reading the market if you can afford the additional risk.

Momentum Trading: generally speaking, momentum trading is a simple sounding strategy that can get complicated fast. When you are using a momentum strategy, you are looking to identify an existing market trend that you expect to continue for some time. While trading using a momentum strategy, use your tools to look for a consistent upward or downward trend - but not, for example, the sort of extreme upward trend you would be looking for under a pure fading strategy.

If you have identified an upward trend, under a momentum strategy, you buy in while the stock is rising, much like under a scalping strategy. Unlike scalping, however, you aren't looking to sell at the minimum point where you can make a profit. Instead, you're aiming to set your price target at the inflection point where the price will begin to fall. This can be done either by monitoring the current prices and charts and selling as soon as you observe momentum shifting, or by setting a price target at a point where you are making a reasonable profit.

If you have identified a downward trend, you can also short under a momentum strategy. Like a normal fade strategy, you are looking to set your price target at a low inflection point where seller volume will decrease, and buyers will begin to re-enter the asset.

Trading the News: trading the news is a specific form of momentum trading that tries to identify an upward or downward trend before it even begins. If you are looking to execute on this strategy, you will be monitoring news headlines for events that will have an effect on a specific stock, a specific business sector, or even the market as a whole. Your goal is to correctly identify a market trend at the point it begins based on that news. This can allow you to increase your profit margin compared to a normal momentum strategy where you are simply buying into an existing trend.

There are regularly occurring, scheduled events that can be helpful to watch out for when trying to execute a news-based strategy. One example would be a publicly traded corporation's quarterly earnings calls. By listening in on an investor earning call, you can try to ascertain whether a company has done better or worse than it was expected to by market analysts. Depending on earnings performance, this can help you identify an upward or downward trend and set your positions early. Another example would be Federal Reserve meetings - the chairman's comments on the market or interest rates can put the entire market into an upward or downward trend on a dime.

Of course, everyone who is trading - especially the large, institutional investors - keeps an eye on scheduled events like this. This means it's hard to get a jump on the news - and big investors will get trades to go through faster than yours ever can. The real opportunities for profit come from unexpected events, or events whose market consequences aren't immediately obvious. If you think you're smarter than the market, maybe you can identify a rise or fall before it happens by taking in all the news you can find. However, betting on uncertain news or nascent trends is risky, and keep that in mind before you take action on an unusual news item.

Range Trading / Daily Pivots: All of the strategies we've discussed so far are somewhat dependent on market conditions where you can discern clear up or down trends in a given asset. However, you can still make money in a very stable market with the strategy of range trading, by taking advantage of the natural, low level volatility that exists in the market - the "noise" or "turbulence" that is always present. Here's a three-step summary of how to execute a range-based strategy:

(1) Identify the daily range of an asset. Your goal in a range strategy is to identify the daily high and low points of the target asset that are caused by natural market volatility, identifying the points of support and resistance that cause price inflection. The easiest way to do this is to pull up a longer-term chart, such as the 4-hour simple moving average, and draw a horizontal line across matching peaks and troughs. The peaks should exist at the point of resistance, where the asset is overbought and demand cannot sustain a higher price. The troughs should exist at points of support -

where the asset is under bought and the supply is insufficient to meet demand at a lower price.

(2) Time your entry so you are buying into the asset when it is priced in the support zone. This is what you expect to be the market low for the day.

(3) Manage your risk. Even though this strategy is looking to take advantage of the predictable volatility in a stable market, you still need to appropriately manage your risk by setting a stop-loss in case you have misjudged the low and set your price target at the expected zone of resistance.

We'll be taking a closer look at one range strategy, commonly referred to as the "day sniper" strategy in

Chapter 5 Demand and Supply and Market Types

The theory of demand and supply is quite interesting and will help you make the right type of investments.

As you know, every stock has its own demand and supply chain, which determines its value. This demand and supply is subject to market volatility and can be a bit hard to predict.

However, understanding the topic will help you predict stock trends to a large extent.

Demand

The demand refers to how many people are interested in buying the stock. As you know, all stocks and financial securities have a certain demand, which is brought about through people's want. If a certain group of people want a particular stock, then its demand will rise. The important thing here is to know what stock has how much demand. You can assess the same by going through news articles and conducting a small research on the market conditions. If you think there is strong demand for a particular stock, then you can consider buying it.

There are various factors that affect the demand of a stock and some are as follows:

Company profile

The name of the company will play a part in determining its demand. Big companies such as Microsoft and apple will have a high demand for their stocks at all times. However, these can be hit by inflation when their values might drop down. On the other hand, there can be some companies whose stock prices will not drop owing to the consistent demand for their goods. For example, Coca-Cola's stock price might not fall in summer despite inflation, as people will buy them at any cost. So, the profile of a company will play a big role in determining its demand.

News

When favorable news breaks about a company, the demand for its stocks rises. If news about a company's merger breaks out, then people will flock to buy its shares. On the other hand, it is also possible for bad news to affect a stock's price positively. So, any news about stocks might help it value rise in the market.

Tastes/ preferences

People's tastes and preferences vary from season to season and might have a significant impact on the demand for a product. Some will prefer to buy certain stocks only during the summer and some during the winter, some during spring etc. These tastes and preferences are hard to predict but can be analyzed through regular research of the markets.

Investor budget

An investor's budget also has a role to play in the overall demand for a commodity. If the investors have a sizeable amount at their disposal then they are sure to create a market and demand for a particular stock. For example, if a high-end investor picks an upcoming company and invests in bulk, then he will immediately create a demand for the company's stock. So, it will help you understand the amount that particular investors have at their disposal.

Future anticipation

In anticipation of a future event, some investors invest in a particular stock in bulk. This will raise the demand for the stock and make it valuable. This generally happens with undervalued stocks and as soon as somebody does the right calculations, others flock to buy the same.

Despite knowing that reasons such as these can affect the prices of stocks, it is still pretty tough to say for sure, how the demand for a stock will fluctuate.

Supply

The supply of a stock is also decided by the investors. Supply refers to having enough to distribute it to whoever is interested in investing. If there are many people wanting the stock but only limited supply then its value will rise. How high it will rise will depend on how many are in need of it and how many sellers are willing to sell.

Supply of stocks is a very important subject to consider while making stock market investments. You will have the chance to look at the number of buyers and sellers for a particular stock when you create a watch list for yourself. If you see that there are more suppliers and only a few buyers, then the stock's value will drop. On the other hand, if there are more buyers and fewer suppliers, then the value of the stock will rise.

You have to sell stock when there are more buyers, and buy stock when there are more sellers, in order to profit from your investments.

Price of stock

The price of a stock will affect its supply. If the price of a particular stock is too high, then demand for it will be low thereby increasing the supply. On the other hand, if the price is low enough for many people to afford, then its supply will be low and its price will rise. So, it is important to understand the price factor variation in order to predict the supply chain of a particular stock.

Price of other stocks

As you know, there will be many stocks floating in the market belonging to various categories. If the price of a particular stock in a particular category changes, then it will impact the price of other stocks in the same category as well! So, it is important to understand how the price of a particular stock will impact the price of another stock.

Government control

The government has control over many stocks and that can significantly impact its prices. The government has limited, nonetheless, powers to affect both the demand and supply of a stock. So, you might have to read up on news about any such policies against certain companies that might affect its stock's supply.

These form some of the factors that can affect the supply of a stock.

Bullish market

A bullish market is better known as an investor's market. The bullish market is quite ideal as the prices of stocks will be on a steady rise. This makes it a lucrative opportunity for investors to invest money in the market.

The term bullish comes from the word bull. Just like how the bull raises its horns in the air to attack its prey, the market lifts up the stocks and flings them in the air. The bullish market is every investor's dream market.

But remember, even if a bullish market exists, it does not guarantee that each and every stock will remain bullish. Some stocks are not affected by the overall market conditions and will follow a course that they have etched for themselves.

Bearish market

A bearish market is the opposite of a bullish market. A bearish market is one where all the prices of stocks are falling. So, it is better known as a seller's market as people will prefer to sell the stocks out of fear of losing out on money.

The bearish market is dreaded by most investors, as it would be risky to make any investment at such a time. However, contrarians will be eager to buy stocks at such points in time.

The term bearish comes from the word bear. Just like how a bear swoops down to attack its prey, the market swoops down on the stocks.

Bullish bar reversal

The bullish bar reversal is one where the days lowest is lower than the previous day's low and the current price is higher than the previous day's high. As soon as this happens, the situation is called a bullish bar reversal. This type is ideal for a stock, as its price pattern will begin to reverse, which means that it will start getting better for the stock. Investors rejoice when such a pattern occurs.

Bearish bar reversal

Bearish bar reversal is the opposite of the bullish bar reversal. Such a situation arises when today's current price is lower than yesterday's closing price. This means that the price of the stock is on a downward trend. This can be because of many reasons and it is best to wait this period out rather than making hasty decisions.

Chapter 6 Developing Your Day Trading Strategy

For new traders, it would be good news to hear that there are many day trading strategies that one can adopt. You can choose to read books such as this or take courses which would train you on the best strategies which you could adopt. Regardless, it is important to understand that trading can be a DIY career. Most successful traders develop strategies which work for them. As such, building your own strategy should always be part of your consideration. In line with this, you shouldn't be convinced that building your own strategy is a challenging task. In fact, once you get down to business, you will notice that it is pretty straightforward. This chapter will take you through the basics of developing your own day trading strategy. Important steps that will be discussed in detail include the process of selecting a market, defining your entry and exit points, evaluating your strategy and ways to enhance your trading strategy.

Market Selection

With the advent of online trading, this has made it possible to have a wide array of financial instruments that traders can depend on. In this case, individuals can trade on other financial instruments besides stocks, futures, and options. Recently, there have been other trading options including the Foreign Exchange Market (forex), Single Stock Futures (SSF) and Exchange Traded Funds (ETFs).

It is worth pointing out that the existing financial securities have been improved to include electronic contracts of notable commodities such as natural gas, gold, silver, grains, and crude oil. These futures are getting popular each day amongst day traders. It is for this reason that pit-traded commodities have been overtaken by the high volume of mini and electronic contracts.

Essentially, the internet has made it possible to trade on anything. Take, for instance, real estates, it is possible to enter this industry without actually owning any properties. This is made possible through Real Estate Investment Trusts (REITs). To understand how you can select an appropriate market to trade, it is imperative to learn about the different markets individually. There are several markets which you could trade in. However, we'll focus on the most popular including stocks, futures, forex and stock options. These markets will be scrutinized based on capital requirements, leverage, liquidity, and volatility.

Capital Requirements

Of course, one of the main considerations that most traders would bear in mind is the amount of capital that they require to initiate their trading activity. Therefore, it is worth examining the markets based on the amount of capital that you would require to begin day trading. Often, experienced traders will recommend the idea of starting small and growing gradually. This gives a novice trader ample time to learn and master the art of day trading.

Leverage

Another essential factor to mull over is leverage. After understanding how to trade on different markets, a trader could always make the best out of the little capital they are using to trade. In this case, leveraged markets give them the opportunity of maximizing their profits by simply using a small amount of capital. Consequently, the advantage gained in using leverage is that a small account can be developed quickly.

Liquidity

Understanding markets based on liquidity is essential. Focusing on liquid markets warrants that traders circumvent the common market issues of slippage and manipulation. Undeniably, any trader would want to make sure that they receive accurate fills for their orders.

Volatility

Without volatility, it would be impossible to make money from different markets. Therefore, markets have to be moving for people to make money. In relation to this, understanding the most volatile market guarantees that a trader puts their money in viable markets.

By now you must be curious to know how markets vary. The following paragraphs will discuss basic information about the different markets you could turn to out there. Undeniably, knowledge is power. Hence, knowing what to expect from these markets is important for any trader.

Trading in Stocks

The thought of trading in stocks scares away many investors. Individuals who have never traded are terrified by the fact that one can easily lose money with wrong decisions. The reality is, stock trading is a risky activity. However, when approached with the right market knowledge, it is an efficient way of building your net worth.

So, what is a stock? A stock is a share. It is also termed as equity. Basically, it is a financial instrument which amounts to ownership in a particular company. When an individual purchases a stock or shares, it means that they own a portion or fraction of the company. For instance, say a trader own 10,000 shares in a company with 100,000 shares. This would mean that the individual has 10% ownership of the stakes. The buyer of such shares is identified as a shareholder. Therefore, the more shares one owns, the larger the proportion of the company which they own. Every time the value of the company shares rise, your share value will also rise. Similarly, if the value falls, your share value also declines. When a company makes a profit, the shareholders are also bestowed with the profits in the form of dividends.

Preferred stock and common stock are the two main types of stocks you should be aware of. The difference that lies between these stocks is that with common stocks, it carries voting rights. This means that a shareholder has an influence in company meetings. Hence, they can have a say in company meetings where the board of directors is elected. On the other hand, preferred shares lack voting rights. However, they are identified as "preferred" shares or stocks because of their preference over common stocks. In the event that a company goes through liquidation, shareholders with preferred shares will be preferred to receive assets or dividends.

Far from the information provided about the varying kinds of stock, a day trader doesn't necessarily have to understand the difference. Remember, you are only a day trader. Thus, you will only buy shares for a short period before selling them within the same day.

Basing on the factors pointed out above, the stock market could be evaluated as follows.

Capital Requirements

According to the Pattern Day Trading Rule, the minimum brokerage balance you are required to maintain for you to trade in stocks is at least $25,000. Without a doubt, this is a lot of money to start with.

Surprisingly, there are tons of traders who began with a lower amount than that. To understand how this rule applies, you need to know what it means to be a pattern day trader. This is the type of trader whereby they execute more than four traders within five business days in their margin accounts.

Leverage

There are two ways of trading in stocks. You could either choose to trade using a margin account or a cash account. With the margin account, it gives a trader the opportunity of buying their stocks on margin. Conversely, with cash accounts, you only buy the stocks for the amount of money present in your account. In other words, you will be trading with a leverage ratio of 1:1.

The notion of trading on margin implies that you will be seeking for funds from your broker. This means that you will be able to buy more stocks far beyond what you can normally afford. To use a margin account, a trader will be required to have at least $2,000 as their starting capital. However, some brokers will demand more. Once your margin account is open, you can get a loan amounting to 50% of the buying price of the stock.

In a real-life example, say you make an initial deposit of $10,000 to your margin account. Since you deposited about 50% of the buying price, it means you are worth twice as much, i.e., $20,000. In other words, your buying power is worth twice what you deposited. Therefore, when you buy stocks worth $5,000, your buying power will reduce to $15,000. Your leverage ratio is therefore 1:2. Traders with a good trading relationship with their brokers could have this ratio increased to even 1:8.

Liquidity

With regards to liquidity, you can be certain that trading in stocks is not a bad idea. There are over 10,000 stocks present in the U.S. stocks exchanges. Most of these stocks are traded on a daily basis. Dealing with these stocks guarantees that you evade the common issues of slippage or manipulation.

Volatility

A trader shouldn't worry about the volatility of the stocks market as they often go through cycles of high and low. This is not a bad thing as a trader simply needs to study when the markets are rising and be wary of instances when markets seem to fall.

Basing on these factors, it would be true to argue that stocks have got good volatility and liquidity. The only issue with stocks is that they have a high capital requirement.

Trading in Forex

Most traders would argue that trading in forex is quite complicated. However, it's not. Just like any other form of trading, you have to stick to the basic rules. In this case, you need to buy when the market is rising and ensure you sell when the market is dropping. Basically, trading in forex involves the process of trading in currencies. In simpler terms, a trader exchanges currency for others based on certain agreed rates. If you have traveled to foreign countries and exchanged your currency against their local currencies, then you should understand how trading in forex works.

At first, it could seem confusing to choose the best currencies, but a trader should simply go for major currencies. Some of the frequently traded currencies include the U.S. dollar, Japanese Yen, European Union Euro, Australian dollar, Canadian dollar, and Swiss franc. An important thing you ought to understand about forex trading is that you need to trade in pairs. This means that when you are buying one currency, you should do this while simultaneously selling another. If you do some digging, you will notice that currencies are quoted in pairs, i.e. USD/JPY or EUR/USD. Below is an

image showing how currencies are quoted in pairs.

Source: "What is a Currency Pair? | ALL Forex Infos."

Often, the most traded forex products include:

- USD/JPY
- EUR/USD
- GBP/USD

An important thing to keep in mind with regards to forex trading is that the market is highly volatile. This means that a trader could easily lose a lot of money within a single day. Before venturing into this market, a trader should take time to understand this market in detail.

The forex market could be evaluated as follows.

Capital Requirements

With the number of brokers over the internet, it is relatively easy to begin forex trading. The best part is that different brokers will require varying amounts of capital from you. Hence, you could settle for the best depending on how much you can afford. You can trade in forex with just $1,000 as your starting capital.

Leverage

Typically, leverage in the forex market stands at 1:100. This implies that if you have $2,000 in your trading account, you can trade $200,000. The ratio varies depending on the forex trader you deal with. There are traders who offer leverage of 1:200.

Liquidity

Liquidity is not an issue in the world of forex trading. The only problem is that a trader doesn't have access to real-time volume data simply because the market is decentralized.

Volatility

Considering the fact that there is high leverage in forex trading, it implies that little movement in the market could earn one huge profit. The market's volatility is quite impressive but not as volatile as the stock market.

Basing on these factors, trading in forex is a smart move. A trader can begin trading with as little as $1,000. Also, with the high leverage present in this market, it is easy to earn huge returns with the right moves.

Trading in Futures

Today, most traders prefer to trade in futures due to its associated advantages. Trading in futures is quite flexible and diverse. The good news is that a trader can employ almost any methodology to trade. Some traders shy away from this form of trading due to their limited knowledge about futures. Also, others are discouraged from trading in futures because they think that it is difficult. Well, to some extent, this is true. Comparing trading in futures to trading in stocks, the former is very risky.

There are different forms of futures contracts including currencies, energies, interest rates, metals, food sector futures, and agricultural futures. The best futures contracts you will find in the market are briefly discussed in the following lines.

S&P 500 E-mini

Most traders will fancy the idea of trading in the S&P 500 E-mini because of its high liquidity aspect. It also appeals to most investors because of its low day trading margins. You can conveniently trade in S&P 500 E-mini around the clock not to mention that you will also benefit from its technical analysis aspect. Essentially, the S&P 500 E-mini is a friendly contract since you can easily predict its price patterns.

10 Year T-Notes

10 Year T-Notes is also ranked as one of the best contracts to trade in. Considering its sweet maturity aspect, most traders would not hesitate to trade in this futures contract. There are low margin requirements that a trader will have to meet when trading in 10 Year T-Notes.

Crude Oil

Crude oil also stands as one of the most popular commodities in futures trading. It is an exciting market because of its high daily trading volume of about 800k. Its high volatility also makes the market highly lucrative.

Gold

This is yet another notable futures contract. It might be expensive to trade in gold; however, it is a great hedging choice more so in poor market conditions.

Capital Requirements

The amount of money required to begin trading in futures will vary. Some brokers will require a trader to have about $5,000. However, there are those who would require only $2,000. It is vital for a trader to choose the best broker who is flexible enough to allow them to trade with the little capital they have.

Leverage

Leverage will also vary depending on the type of futures you trade in. The contract value will also have an impact on the amount of leverage that you will have.

Liquidity

Just like leverage, the liquidity aspects of futures will also depend on the futures you are trading. Accordingly, it is important for any trader to regularly check the respective volumes of contracts before trading on them.

Volatility

Futures are volatile. The advantage gained by using high leverage ensures that a trader makes good profit with little price changes in the market.

Keeping the above factors into consideration, futures are a good market to trade. A trader can easily day trade with as little as $2,000. The high leverage ratio will also guarantee that huge profits can be earned.

Trading in Stock Options

Trading in stock options is almost similar to trading in futures. Here, a trader also buys stocks at a pre-established price and later sells when prices rise.

Capital Requirements

Stock options trading also affected by the Pattern Day Trading Rule. This means that your minimum capital requirements will be $25,000. If you engage in more than four trades in a particular week, then you should have about $30,000 in your trading account.

Leverage

Since there are many options to choose from, leverage will vary. The exciting aspect of stock options is that they have high leverage amounts.

Liquidity

With regards to liquidity, stock options are not that liquid. A keen eye on this market reveals that a few options are traded on a regular basis. The low volume of trades is affected by the many options that traders can choose from. Fortunately, stock options are rarely manipulated by the market. Their values are not influenced by supply and demand.

Volatility

Stock options are highly volatile.

From the look of things, stock options have similar pros and cons like trading in stocks. Most new traders will shy away from this form of day trading due to its high capital demands. Its high volatility could be scary to most investors as it makes the market to be unpredictable. This makes this form of trading to be very risky. Therefore, it is not recommended for new traders.

Selecting a Trading Timeframe

Obviously, day trading will require you to choose a timeframe which is less than a day. It is worth noting that the time frame you choose will have an impact on the profit you make. For instance, if you choose a time frame which is less than 60 minutes, the chances are that your profits will be lower. If you trade using a larger time frame, it will increase your chances of getting more profits.

With smaller time frames, you get smaller profits. Nonetheless, the advantage here is that you lower your risks too. This means that if you are new to trading, smaller time frames would be a smart choice. There are pros and cons of short and long-term frames. You simply need to make a choice based on your financial goals. The best way to make your selection is by experimenting with varying timeframes. If your strategy doesn't work with a small timeframe, you could switch to a larger timeframe.

Defining Your Entry Trigger

Besides knowing the right market to trade in, you also need to know when to enter the market. Candlestick and bar patterns are ideal triggers to use. The following image shows you how the triggers will look like.

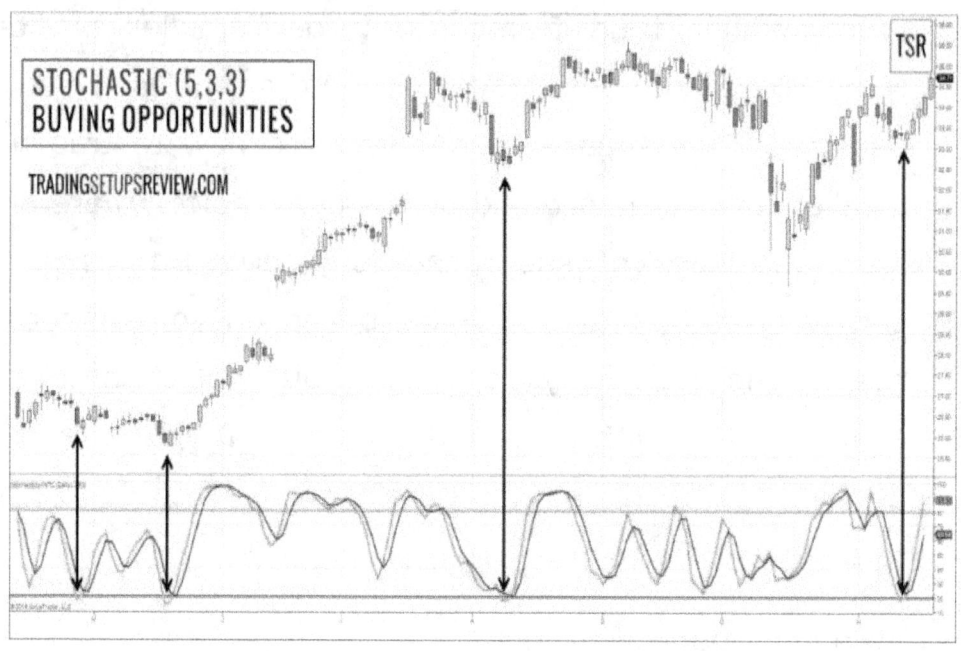

Source: "10 Steps To Creating Your First Trading Strategy."

Knowing Your Exit Trigger

Certainly, with day trading, anything can go wrong. There are times when markets will quickly drop which could affect your returns. Knowing when to exit is therefore important. Essentially, exiting is not just about selling when things don't go your way. You also need to exit when things are going as you expected. This ensures that you make the best out of your investment. You should always set your feelings aside as the market will not always be on your side. Know when to stop at the right times.

Define Your Risk

After knowing when to enter and exit the market, you need to know how much risk you can stomach. The best way of doing this is by position sizing. Position sizing helps you to know the amount of money you are ready to risk. If you double your position size, it means that you will also double your risk. Always ensure that you decide your position size wisely.

Know Your Trading Rules

At the beginning of your trading activity, you will notice that the trading rules you use are simple. In fact, you can memorize some of these rules. Regardless, it is recommended that you write your rules down. This is a practical method which guarantees you maintain discipline throughout your trading activity.

Constantly Improve Your Trading Strategy

Your trading strategy will not always bring you profits. This is normal since your strategy is not static. As you continue trading, you will gain knowledge and experience. Therefore, you need to find a way of also improving your trading strategy. When doing this, you should, however, adjust the strategy gradually and not drastically.

In a nutshell, having a trading strategy is vital for the success of your trading business. You should strive to use a trading strategy which you are comfortable with. With regards to choosing the right market to trade, also ensure that you make your choice based on your financial goals. Don't just pick a market because most people are trading there. Your decision should be based solely on what you think works for you.

Chapter 7 Trading *Psychology*

Throughout this book, we have discussed how psychological factors affect investors' behavior. Often, investors may choose to act in a cautious manner, while other times investors may choose to go in headfirst.

Also, psychology tends to wreak havoc on the average investor. This is especially true when investors are new to trading and get sucked in by the trends in markets. For instance, new investors may be driven to the siren's song of a "hot" stock. This can lead to a poor decision, in which the stock may rapidly drop in value, leaving the investor with heavy losses.

Other times, investors may be sucked in by a bubble.

A bubble is nothing more than an artificially-inflated price for an asset.

Thus, bubbles form when investors lose sight of the true value of an asset and get taken in by the actions of other investors. Since some investors decide to keep driving the price of an asset up higher and higher, they may end up doing more harm than good to the average investor. The average investor may then become drawn in by the potential of higher gain.

The problem with bubbles is that if the underlying asset is not really as hot is it might seem, then the price of that asset may come crashing back down to Earth. As we saw earlier, asset prices tend to revert back to their trend, unless they meet new resistance levels.

However, determining whether or not an asset has found a new resistance level is hard to predict and is often related to observing its 2-day, 10-day, and 50-day trends. When observing the trend of the price of an asset, it becomes easier to see where the asset's price is headed. As such, an investor may see a downward trend and may figure that a spike in its price is not justified.

On the other hand, the price of an asset may be trending upward, and the dip in its price is just an outlier. So, an investor may choose to do what is known as "buying on the dip". In this case, the investor is banking on the asset's price returning to its mean and therefore a higher price.

In these examples, bubbles are fueled by irrational expectations, which eventually lead to disappointment and potential losses.

Think of real estate markets.

Some cities in North America are in "housing bubbles"—that is, prices getting higher and higher. People are willing to pay more and more to get into a specific area. Those who cannot afford to get into that area are forced to watch from the sidelines.

The problem with housing bubbles is that markets turn on a dime and can leave homeowners with large mortgages while the value of their properties is slashed. This makes it virtually impossible to sell the property, as the sale price may not even cover the remaining amount of the mortgage. This leaves folks stuck with paying for an overpriced home in hopes of the market turning once again.

So, this is why a recurring theme is this book is about doing research and understanding the dynamics of each market.

The Fear of Missing Out

Investors also may run into a phenomenon known as the "fear of missing out". This concept refers to the fact that some folks are so concerned about missing out on opportunities that they choose to "get in on the ground floor" of an investment which may not be going anywhere.

This is especially true with IPOs.

Some investors may miss out on an IPO and regret having missed out. So, they vow to catch the next great IPO. Sure enough, an opportunity pops up. The investor, often without doing their due diligence, decides to go head first into the IPO. They sink considerable amounts of funds into the IPO.

Unfortunately, the IPO was hyped up too much, and investors are lukewarm about it. The IPO gains some traction but then fizzles out. The investor is then disappointed, because they didn't make the amount of money they had hoped to make.

In the best of cases, they might end up making less than expected on the IPO. In the worst of cases, they may end up losing money on the deal. Had the investor been rational, they may have sunk less into the deal or perhaps avoided it altogether.

This is why managing expectations, especially when the fear of losing out is prevalent, is of the utmost importance. Those investors who do not take care with managing their expectations may be tempted to try to hit a home run on a single pitch. While it is possible to hit a home run, it may not be as easy as one might think. Thus, investors need to keep a level head, especially when the market is red hot.

Herd Mentality

One other concept which has been presented earlier in this book is "herd mentality". This is when investors rush into an investment or asset class because everyone else is doing so.

You often hear this with gold and silver. You hear calls of so-called experts claiming the end of the world is near, and you must load up on gold and silver, in order to protect your wealth from Armageddon.

So, investors heed the warnings and go head first into gold and silver without actually studying the valuation mechanism for this asset class. As the price goes up, individual investors become worried that they will miss the boat. They are willing to pay ever-increasing prices.

As the herd begins to gobble up more gold and more silver, others join in, as they fear the worst is yet to come. In the end, the world does not end, and the price of precious metals falls. Investors are left with stockpiles of gold and silver, which fall below the price they originally paid. While this doesn't mean that the metals are worthless, investors will feel cheated and disappointed, because the funds allocated to the purchase of these metals could have been better invested elsewhere.

This example underscores the problem with following the crowd. So, when you see folks running in one direction, always ask yourself what it is they are running from. If you can figure why they are running, it might even be a better investment for you to go where they are running from than to follow the crowd.

Chapter 8 Support or Resistance Trading

Horizontal trade or resistance trade is the preferred negotiation style. The market knows no diagonals. It is reminiscent of the price level – the logic reason of horizontal support or resistance levels. However, the diagonal trend lines are deceiving and open to subjectivity – a reason to not use it as it can lead to bias, fraud, and illusions. Diagonal trend lines are the most unreliable implements. It traces false lines that can affect prices, movement, slope, and implication. For example, having an attempt to buy can make you draw a trend line a little more abruptly.

Support is a level of price where the purchase is solid enough to reverse a bearish trend. When a bearish trend finds resistance, it runs like a top marathon that reaches the finish line and then continuously moving away from it. The resistance level is denoted by a horizontal line in a diagram that connects more than two lines.

Resistance is a level of price where the sale is tough enough to reverse an up-trend. An uptrend that acquires support is like a person who accidentally bumped by a moving car when he crosses the street then eventually stopped and collapsed. The supported is denoted by a horizontal line on a diagram that connects more than two upper parts.

A slight support or resistance will cause the trends to continue while reversing through strong support or resistance. The traders tend to buy support while others sell against the resistance turning its value into rewarding foresight.

Summary of the Support or Resistance Trading

1. Each morning, when you create your daily watch list, look immediately at the day cards on your watch list and find the support or resistance area.
2. Control the price action in these areas in a 5-minute chart. If an indecisive candle is formed in this area, this is the level confirmation, and you enter the operation. Generally, to minimize the risk, you should buy closely as possible. The stop is your pause and should be done no more than 5 minutes under the support or resistance levels.
3. Advances are to expect on the next support or resistance levels.
4. Don't close your trade not unless it already reached its profit aim or extends another support or resistance levels.

5. **Selling positions are commonly happening close the profit aim or support or resistance levels. Then, you set your stop to reach the entry or breakeven point.**

6. Closing your shares nearby to the middle position of cash level when there are no evident of support or resistance levels.

Develop Your Strategy

You must still find your place in the market. You may be a 1-minute or a 5-minute trader; you may be a 60-minute trader. Some may be daily or weekly traders (swing traders). There's a place in the market for everyone. Consider what you are learning in this book as pieces of a puzzle that together make up the bigger picture of trading. You're going to acquire some pieces here; you're going to pick up pieces on your own from your reading and research, and, overall, you will create a puzzle that will develop into your unique trading strategy. This book will help you develop a strategy that is going to work for you, your personality, your account size and your risk tolerance.

The key is that you master a strategy. Once you have a strategy in the market, you can become a trader without breaking your bank account. This is more than sitting on a chair. Remember that the more time spent looking at your chart, the further you will learn. It is a kind of job where you survive until you can do it. You can start throwing later, but first, you must master only one strategy. It can be the exchange of VWAP, it can be a bullish indicator momentum strategy, it can be a reversal strategy, or it can create its own strategy. Reduce the options, convert this area of strength into a viable strategy and use that strategy to survive until you can develop others.

It is absolutely crucial for each trader to act on a strategy. Plan an exchange and change the plan. You have to act a strategy. If you exchange real money, you must have a written strategy and historical data to verify that it is worth trading with real money. You cannot change your plan if you have already entered the operation and have an open position.

The truth about traders is that they fail. They lose money, and a large percentage of those traders are not getting the education that you are receiving from this book. They're going to be using live trading strategies that are not even hammered out, they will be haphazardly trading a little of this and a little of that until their account is gone, and then they will wonder what happened.

You don't want to live trade a new strategy until you've proven that it's worth investing in. You may practice three months on a simulator, and then trade small size with real money for one month, and then go back to the simulator to work on your mistakes or practice new strategies for another three months. There is no shame in going back to a simulator at any stage of your day trading career. Even experienced and professional traders, when they want to develop a new strategy, test it out on a live simulator first.

Your focus, while reading this book and practicing in simulated accounts, should be to develop a strategy worth trading, and it's my pleasure to assist you with that process. Remember, the market is always going to be there. You don't need to rush this. A day trading career is a marathon and not a sprint. It's not about making $50,000 by the end of next week. It's about developing a set of skills that will last a lifetime.

Successful Trading Guide and Money Management

The philosophy in the business is that you only have to master a few solid configurations to be consistently profitable. In fact, a simple trading method, which consists of a few minimal configurations, confusion and stress helps reduce and allows you to focus more on the psychological aspect of the negotiation, which really distinguishes the winners from the losers.

Now that you have learned the basics of some business strategies let's take a closer look at the actual planning and negotiation process. Now understand the configuration you want to act, but as a beginner trader, you will have a difficult time in advance to plan a trade and start. It is very common to have a good set-up, but then go into a trade at the wrong time or let the money go and at the same time make money from others. I think the solution is to develop a process for your trade. Plan an exchange and change a plan.

Trading process:

- Routine morning activities
- Create an observation list
- Consolidate a negotiation plan
- Start the trade accordingly
- Implementation and execution of plans
- Diary and reflection

You must remember that what makes an operation profitable is the correct execution of all the steps in the previous process. Write your reasons for entering and leaving each operation. Everyone can read this book or dozens of other books, but few people have the discipline to function properly. You may have a good configuration, but choose an incorrect action to trade. An action manipulated by computers and institutional traders. You may find an appropriate action to negotiate but negotiate at the wrong time. A bad entry will ruin your plan, and eventually, you will lose your money. You can find a good stock for trade and enter a trade properly, but if you do not get the right one, it will become an unprofitable trade, a loss of decisions. All the steps of the process are important.

Think about something important that you often do in your life and then think about how you can do better. Now think about how you are doing right now. This is a great mind process for traders. When making an exchange, you must make sure you focus on the right things, before you start and negotiate. Forming a system for this proper process will eliminate majority of the emotional dependencies that traders encounter when they try to get in and manage an operation.

Final Rule

Profitable trade should not encompass any emotional aspect. If you are a sensitive trader, you will lose your money.

Training and practice give you an overview of what is involved in the action, how you act and how you can grow and develop your skills. Once you have a perspective of what matters, you can continue to identify the specific processes on which you should focus. The key to success is the exact knowledge of their processes. You often learn them the hard way, losing money.

Sticking to your negotiation plan and the discipline inherent in your negotiation methodology have caused a snowball effect positive habits in your life in general, and these habits have contributed to more commercial success.

Yes, snowball effect of positive habits. Day trading requires practice, routine, and development of positive habits. If you make a conscious effort in day trading, you will become an effective and successful trader in time.

For example, start your negotiation actions by following the same routine when you wake up in the sunrise. You always do a race in the morning before the negotiation session begins. For example, you live in Vancouver, Canada, and the market opens at 6:30, your time. You wake up every morning at 5 o'clock. You go from 5 to 5:45 p. M. (Usually between 7 and 10 kilometers (or 4 to 6 miles)). You come home, you shower and at 6 o'clock you begin to develop your plan.

If your body was not active before operating, you would make bad decisions. There are scientific studies that show that aerobic exercise has a positive effect on the decision-making process. People who regularly participate in aerobic exercise (e.g., at least 30 minutes) have higher values for neuropsychological functions and performance tests of cognitive functions, such as attention control, inhibition control, flexibility cognitive, working memory update and the speed of processing capacity and the measurement of information.

In day trading, it is not enough to be better than the average. You have to surpass the crowd to win in the daily trade. Regrettably, most of the people who were attracted to day trading are the impulsive, plungers, and selfish ones – those who think that the world should provide them more than what they have.

This reality does not mean to say you have to be like or act like them. Note that in order to win, you need to develop self-discipline. Your mindset and behavior are far different from the losers. Analyze yourself, disregard the deceptions, and change your old negative ways. I understand that in a way it is difficult, however, if you want to succeed in day trading, you need to work hard for it. You need not only to learn how day trading works but to improve your behavior and personality too. A successful trader is smart, motivated, and focused.

Now let's go back to the negotiation: as already mentioned, trade cannot be considered a hobby. You have to take the trade seriously. So you get up at 5 in the morning, you walk for 30 to 45 minutes, you shower, you dress, and you eat porridge for breakfast before you start your trading session at 6 in the morning.

. You are awake, alert and motivated when you sit down and start building your watch list. This morning, the routine of your mental preparation has tremendously helped you get to the market. So, whatever you do, the morning starts in a similar way to paying invaluable dividends. Waking up and washing your face with water 15 minutes in advance will give you little time to prepare for the opening of the market. Sitting on the computer in pajamas or underwear does not make you attack the market.

Your follow-up list comes from a standard analysis that you use every morning. You will be less likely to get mixed up to other stuff because you are sure that the stock of this scanner has the best chance of operating. Review each action, in the same way, using a checklist to see if it really is marketable to you. Your watch list will be created at 6:15 a.m. and will not add anything after that time since there will not be enough time to review new stocks and plan an operation. So you can see the tickers on our watch list 15 minutes before the opening. This really takes you to another step in your process.

In the 15 minutes prior to opening, you will see the tickers on your watch list and develop trading plans for them based on the price action you see. This is the most difficult part and requires experience, knowledge, and education. Many traders fail in this step.

When the bell rings at 6:30 a.m., your plans are recorded in the notebooks because it can be so easily missed out each of the open ticker you saw.

What is your next move if it is set on the long one? How about your next move if it turns out the opposite? What are your assumptions on the actions you made? How feasible are profit aims? What part should you establish your stop? Does your profit frame good enough to negotiate? If you ask these questions when planning your exchange, you have a clear advantage, because then you can continue and follow a battle plan. If it's close to your face, you can easily emphasize it, and that will eliminate the fear you felt when the bell rang. All you do in the opening is find your signal and activate the exchange.

Upon checking your watch list, you saw that Sarepta Therapeutics Inc (NASDAQ: SRPT) had a 15% difference. They knew that interest in buying shares was low. Who would dare to buy if shares fell overnight by 15%? In fact, most investors are trying to go out and sell before it goes down as if there is something really bad about the company. They could not find support or resistance in the vicinity, so opt for VWAP and choose a short VWAP operation.

Once the stock is configured, an entry is signaled and activated; you will enter without questioning (well, that is the plan). Sometimes you can appreciate yourself, but not too often. You have set my profit objectives in your trading plan, as well as the technical level at which you will be going to your stops, so after entering, concentrate only on my brands and your reservation benefit.

There are some who say that the hardest part of negotiating is knowing when to leave. It can be very difficult to stop trading too soon if you do not have an established plan. If you have a plan in advance and you meet it, you are more likely to make your payroll work and reduce your losses quickly, rather than the opposite. This is also useful to keep your emotions in check during the trade.

Once the exchange is over, you will think about how well your plan worked and how well you have done what you wrote. Most of your exchanges will be considered at night when you review and recap your operations from that day. You should ask yourself: "Which part did I do well?", "Are there any mistakes I have done?" And "Should I have sold myself before?" These are utterly crucial questions for the buildup of your trade.

Be noted that there is fact that even if you have obtained good profits, that still does not mean that you are an excellent trader.

Being a good trader is able to determine the importance of both sides of the table.

First write or take a video summary of the trade and everything that comes to mind at your school, then combine it with other previous lessons and use them all as a reference for the future. Some lessons are more difficult compared to others, but rest assured that it will only improve over time. You just need some time to absorb all the knowledge and details, and then implement them

Why is this trade process important? This process is important because it describes how things are prepared for an operation and then keep the focus for execution. It helps filter social, emotional noise and gives you a better sight for a more rewarding victory.

As long you keep focus and implement on the right processes, you may be on the right path to trading success.

Chapter 9 Fibonacci Trading Strategy

Fibonacci numbers start with 0 and 1 and then increase exponentially from there by adding the 2 previous numbers together to get the next number in the sequence. As such it starts off with 0, 1, 2, 3, 5 and so on and so forth. The difference between these numbers is known as the Fibonacci ratio which includes .236, .382, .5 and so on and so forth. Finding these ratios in the pairs you are considering allows you to determine naturally occurring entry and exit points.

Using the Fibonacci sequence to perform a retracement gives you the ability to determine how much an asset moved in price initially. It uses multiple horizontal lines to point out resistance or support at either 23.6, 38.2, 50, 61.8 or 100 percent. When used properly they make it easier to identify the spots transactions should be started, what prices to target and what stop losses to set.

This doesn't mean that you should apply the Fibonacci retracements blindly as doing so can lead to failure as easily as it can success. It is important to avoid choosing inconsistent reference points which can easily lead to mistakes as well as misanalysis, for example, mistaking the wick for the body of a candle. Retracements using the Fibonacci sequence should always be applied wick-to-wick which in turn leads to a clearly defined and actionable resistance level.

Likewise, it is important to always keep the big picture in mind and keep an eye on trends that are of the longer variety as well. Failing to keep the broad perspective in mind makes short-term trades more likely to fail as it makes it harder to project the correct momentum and direction any potential opportunities might be moving in. Keeping the larger trends in mind will help you pick more reliable trades while also preventing you from accidentally trading against a specific trend.

Don't forget, Fibonacci retracements are likely to indicate quality trades, but they will never be able to do so in a complete vacuum. It is best to start with a retracement and then apply other tools including stochastic oscillators or MACD. Moving ahead without confirmation will leave you with little except positive thoughts and wishes that the outcome goes the way you want. Remember, there is no one indicator that is strong enough to warrant moving forward on a trade without double checking the validity of the data.

The other limitation of a Fibonacci retracement is that it doesn't work reliably over shorter time frames as there is simply too much interference from standard market volatility which will result in false apparent levels of support as well as resistance. What's more, the addition of whipsaws and spikes can make it difficult to utilize stops effectively which can result in tight and narrow confluences.

While a singular Fibonacci retracement can be meaningful on its own from time to time, two or more Fibonacci retracements or extensions that show the same thing are almost always going to lead to viable results. The concept of overlapping Fibonacci retracements is one that most traders discover on their own over time. It commonly includes the use of other types of retracements or extensions with the purpose of determining a variety of signals including support and resistance levels as well as relevant pivot points.

As such, a group of overlapping retracements is a significant improvement as two strong Fibonacci levels are all that are required in order to determine a reliable trade in many cases. Specifically, the presence of a pair of Fibonacci levels at a point of known resistance or support is almost always enough to yield viable results. The simplicity of this strategy is one of its greatest strengths and many traders use it to the exclusion of all else when trading in the forex market.

Using this strategy: When it comes to utilizing this strategy correctly, you can use any chart that you like as long as it contains either a run down or a run up of a given currency price in addition to multiple retracements. From there, you will need to begin adding Fibonacci lines to the chart. If you draw these Fibonacci lines on a powerful down trend, then you will be able to start from the high point on the chart before moving toward the lowest swing point. If you are following an uptrend, then the reverse is going to be true. Once this is done you will need to find the confluence points that comes from any Fibonacci level including 38 percent, 50 percent, 62 percent and 79 percent.

Fibonacci extensions: To use Fibonacci extensions with this strategy, the basics are going to be more or less the same. You are simply going to choose the chart of your choice before adding in the Fibonacci lines with the Fibonacci extensions enabled as well. A particularly useful time to utilize this strategy is when the market is ranging between the support and resistance levels. It doesn't matter if the actual range is long or short, it will eventually break because the market cannot stay in an indecisive position forever.

The best way to determine the direction that a ranging market is going to break in is by first determining the range on the timeframe you are considering before then determining the low and the high based on that range. If the Fibonacci levels indicate that the price is going to break above the range, then the uptrend is likely going to form and if it breaks below the range then a downtrend is likely to form. While this will allow you to more accurately determine the next major movement that is likely to occur, it is still important to wait for that instance to actually come to pass before you move to take advantage of it.

On the other hand, you may instead want to wait for the range to break out once, before getting in on the second wave. This is frequently a good idea as a vast majority of traders spend time waiting for the initial break, regardless of how far away it may be in the moment. What's more, when this does occur, the price moves a great deal in a very short period of time, causing most of these traders to close out which drops the price, which a third round of traders is then happy to take advantage of.

These first three waves typically happen quite quickly before a much larger fourth wave of traders swoops in after they finally get on board with what is actually happening. As such, the most profitable time to get in is during the third wave as you avoid paying a premium while still expecting a fair amount of the profits you would see if you managed to get in any earlier.

In order to take advantage of this movement, you are going to want to determine the initial range breakout before waiting for the price to start moving against it. You will then want to wait some more and have the price return to moving in the breakout direction once again. Once this occurs you are going to want to take the proper position and set the target to the low support line with a stop above the 0.0 level.

At this point, you will need to wait for the price to break past the lowest support line as if this does not occur then you are going to want to close out your position and try your luck again the next time the price starts following the trade in question. If the price does ultimately break through the lower support line, then you are going to wait for it to retest the broken support so that you can confidently close out your position before waiting for the price to once more come into alignment with the trend. Once it breaks past the support line but fails to crest above it, then you are going to want to take the relevant position based on the trend and set a level of 161.80 as the new target.

Assuming the trend breaks at this point and presents itself in such a way that it appears as though it is strong enough to continue to 423.60 then you will want to ensure you have the proper position and set this as your target while putting the stop loss slightly above 261.80.

Mistakes to avoid

While Fibonacci levels can provide a great deal of insight into the trading process, it can also lead to serious issues and massive losses if used incorrectly. As such, you are going to want to be aware of the following commonly made mistake sin order to ensure that your strategy works out according to plan.

Avoid mixing reference points: In order to correctly fit your retracements to the relevant price action, you are always going to want to keep steady reference points. This means that if you are using a low trend as a reference past the close of a session or in the body of a candle, then your ideal high price should always be visible in the candle at the top of the trend. Mistake and misanalysis can make it easy to accidentally skew these reference points by moving from the wick to the body of the candle hurting your potential for profit in the process. Luckily, consistently holding on to your reference points will also make it easier for you to determine accurate support and resistance levels at the moment.

Avoid ignoring long-term trends: If you get in the habit of dealing with short term charts then it can be easy to lose focus on the big picture. This narrowing of your perspective can ultimately result in misguided short-term trades if you aren't careful. Keeping a close eye on long-term trends, even if you don't plan on actively trading them can help you determine if the short-term trends you have found are all that they appear cracked up to be. Even better, this level of perception will allow you to potentially act on trends that have a great deal of momentum turning a solid 50 pip profit into one that is 400 pips or more.

Chapter 10 Finding Entry and Exit Points

We've talked quite a bit about support and resistance levels and now it's time to turn a little more attention to them. Understanding these twin concepts and how they predict market behavior is crucial to knowing when to get in and out of the market. In this chapter, we'll get

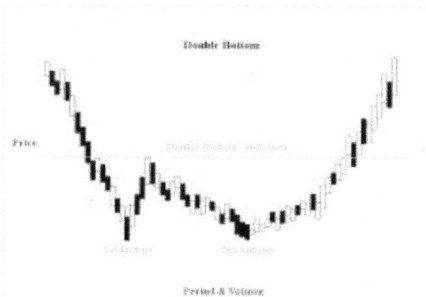

further into what these forces do and how to spot them.

The chart above is a good example of support. Look at the two low points, or "bottoms," on the chart. These are points where the price tends to rebound. Once you've calculated a support level, you can expect the price to "bounce" off of it.

Proactive Calculations

Using pivot point calculations, whether your own or from a technical analysis source you trust, is usually the starting point for finding support and resistance levels. Pivot point levels are called "proactive" support or resistance, as opposed to "reactive." What this means is that it is predictive of future behavior, rather than describing current behavior. Remember that no prediction is perfect, and the calculation methods may be proven incorrect. There is a margin of error expected in calculating resistance and support, but if the price continues its motion through the pivot calculation point, that means that a new top or bottom is being found. When this happens, the previous point frequently remains a point of resistance or support, but to a lesser degree. Proactive support and resistance calculations are not set in stone. Rather than reading them as gospel, treat them as guidelines. They'll give you information about where to set your stops, where you should keep a close watch on your assets, and how to calculate your potential reward/risk ratios. Get comfortable with this math because you'll be using it every day.

Reactive Support

An example of reactive support is the candlestick

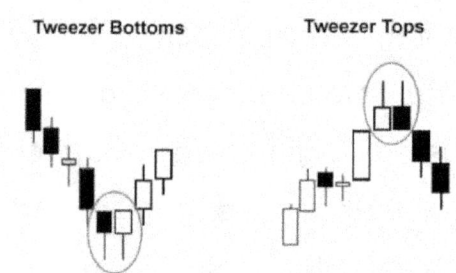

pattern known as "tweezers."

As you can see, they show a reversal in momentum that has already happened. When this stock history shows this pattern repeatedly at a certain price point, this is undoubtedly a marker of resistance or support at that level.

Trendlines

Over time, you may see that support and resistance levels change in a predictable pattern over time. We'll use support as an example, but it works exactly the same way for resistance levels. Let's say that the price of stock XYZ has bounced back up at $80 per share, then $75 per share, then $70 per share. If you were to draw a line through these support levels, you would see that the line trends upward, meaning that support is rising. If your pivot calculation gave you a likely support level at $65 for this stock on this day, you could be very confident in that calculation because it was supported by the trendline. If your pivot calculation was coming to $80 though, you might place slightly less faith in the calculation because it contradicts your trendline.

Round Numbers

An interesting psychological fact about support and resistance levels is how neatly they seem to place themselves at prices ending with "50" and "00." This is entirely due to the fact that people like round numbers and respect them more than other numbers when deciding whether to buy or sell stocks. Practically, this means that if there is a support or resistance at round number, it is much less likely that the price will punch through that level and break out of the prediction.

Chapter 11 Portfolio Diversification

Day traders generally execute trades in the course of a single trading day while investors buy and hold stocks for days, weeks, months, and sometimes even a couple of years. In between these two extremes are other forms of trading. These include swing trading and position trading, among others.

Swing trading is where a trader buys an interest in a commodity or stock and holds the position for a couple of days before disposing of it. Position trading, on the other hand, is where a trader buys a stake in a commodity or stock for a number of weeks or even several months. While all these trades carry a certain element of risk, day trading carries the biggest risk.

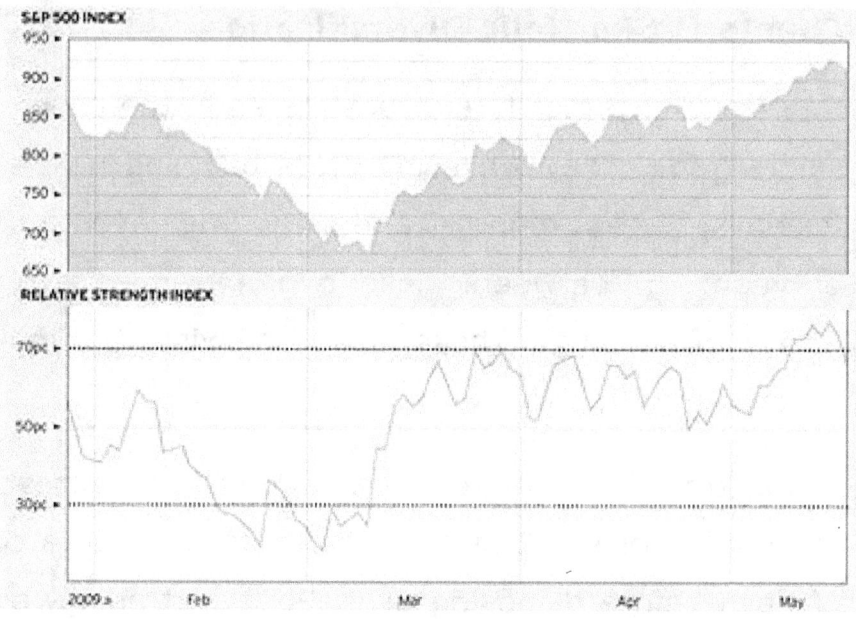

A trader with the necessary skills and access to all the important resources is bound to succeed and will encounter a steep learning curve. Professional day traders work full time, whether working for themselves or for large institutions. They often set a schedule which they always adhere to. It is never wise to be a part-time day trader, a hobby trader, or a gambler. To succeed, you have to trade on a full-time basis and be as disciplined as possible.

Introduction to Diversification

Diversification is considered an effective risk management technique. It is widely used by both traders and investors. The gist behind this approach is that investing funds in just single security is extremely risky as the entire trade could potentially go up in smoke or incur significant losses.

An ideal portfolio of securities is expected to fetch a much higher return compared to a no-diversified portfolio. This is true even when compared to the returns of lower risk investments like bonds. Generally, diversification is advisable not only because it yields better returns but also because it offers protection against losses.

Diversification Basics

Traders and investors put their funds in securities at the securities markets. One of the dangers of investing in the markets is that traders are likely to hold onto only one or two stocks at a time. This is risky because if a trade was to fail, then the trader could experience a catastrophe. However, with diversification, the risk is spread out so that regardless of what happens to some stocks, the trader still stands to be profitable.

At the core of diversification is the challenge posed by unsystematic risks. When some stocks or investments perform better than others, these risks are neutralized. Therefore, for a perfectly balanced portfolio, a trader should ensure that they only deal with assets that are non-correlated. This means that the assets respond in opposite ways or differently to market forces.

The ideal portfolio should contain between 25 and 30 different securities. This is the perfect way of ensuring that the risk levels are drastically reduced and the only expected outcomes are profitability.

In summary, diversification is a popular strategy that is used by both traders and investors. It makes use of a wide variety of securities in order to improve yield and mitigate against inherent and potential risks.

It is advisable to invest or trade in a variety of assets and not all from one class. For instance, a properly diversified portfolio should include assets such as currencies, options, stocks, bonds, and so on. This approach will increase the chances of profitability and minimize risks and exposure. Diversification is even better if assets are acquired across geographical regions as well.

Best Diversification Approach

Diversification focuses on asset allocation. It consists of a plan that endeavors to allocate funds or assets appropriately across a variety of investments. When an investor diversifies his or her portfolio, then there is some level of risk that has to be accepted. However, it is also advisable to devise an exit strategy so that the investor is able to let go of the asset and recoup their funds. This becomes necessary when a specific asset class is not yielding any worthwhile returns compared to others.

If an investor is able to create an aptly diversified portfolio, their investment will be adequately covered. An adequately diversified portfolio also allows room for growth. Appropriate asset allocation is highly recommended as it allows investors a chance to leverage risk and manage any possible portfolio volatility because different assets have varying reactions to adverse market conditions.

Investor opinions on diversifications

Different investors have varying opinions regarding the type of investment scenarios they consider being ideal. Numerous investors believe that a properly diversified portfolio will likely bring in a double-digit return despite prevailing market conditions. They also agree that in the worst case situation will be simply a general decrease in the value of the different assets. Yet with all this information out there, very few investors are actually able to achieve portfolio diversification.

So why are investors unable to simply diversify their portfolios appropriately? The answers are varied and diverse. The challenges encountered by investors in diversification include weighting imbalance, hidden correlation, underlying devaluation, and false returns, among others. While these challenges sound rather technical, they can easily be solved. The solution is also rather simple. By hacking these challenges, an investor will then be able to benefit from an aptly diversified platform.

The Process of Asset Class Allocation

There are different ways of allocating investments to assets. According to studies, most investors, including professional investors, portfolio managers, and seasoned traders actually rarely beat the indexes within their preferred asset class. It is also important to note that there is a visible correlation between the performance of an underlying asset class and the returns that an investor receives. In general, professional investors tend to perform more or less the same as an index within the same class asset.

Investment returns from a diversified portfolio can generally be expected to closely imitate the related asset class. Therefore, asset class choice is considered an extremely crucial aspect of an investment. In fact, it is the single more crucial aspect for the success of a particular asset class. Other factors, such as individual asset selection and market timing, only contribute about 6% of the variance in investment outcomes.

Wide Diversifications between Various Asset Classes Diversification to numerous investors simply implies spreading their funds through a wide variety of stocks in different sectors such as health care, financial, energy, as well as medium caps, small, and large-cap companies. This is the opinion of your average investor. However, a closer look at this approach reveals that investors are simply putting their money in different sectors of stocks class. These asset classes can very easily fall and rise when the markets do.

A reliably diversified portfolio is one where the investor or even the manager is watchful and alert because of the hidden correlation that exists between different asset classes. This correlation can easily change with time, and there are several reasons for this. One reason is international markets. Many investors often choose to diversify their portfolios with international stocks.

However, there is also a noticeable correlation across the different global financial markets. This correlation is clearly visible not just across European markets but also emerging markets from around the world. There is also a clear correlation between equities and fixed income markets, which are generally the hallmarks of diversification.

This correlation is actually a challenge and is probably a result of the relationship between structured financing and investment banking. Another factor that contributes to this correlation is the rapid growth and popularity of hedge funds. Take the case where a large international organization such as a hedge fund suffers losses in a particular asset class.

Should this happen, then the firm may have to dispose of some assets across the different asset classes. This will have a multiplier effect as numerous other investments, and other investors will, therefore, be affected even though they had diversified their portfolios appropriately. This is a challenge that affects numerous investors who are probably unaware of its existence. They are also probably unaware of how it should be rectified or avoided.

Realignment of Asset Classes

One of the best approaches to solving the correlation challenge is to focus on class realignment. Basically, asset allocation should not be considered as a static process. Asset class imbalance is a phenomenon that occurs when the securities markets develop, and different asset classes exhibit varied performance.

After a while, investors should assess their investments then diversify out of underperforming assets and instead shift this investment to other asset classes that are performing well and are profitable in the long term. Even then, it is advisable to be vigilant so that no one single asset class is over-weighted as other standard risks are still inherent. Also, a prolonged bullish market can result in overweighting one of the different asset classes which could be ready for a correction. There are a couple of approaches that an investor can focus on, and these are discussed below.

Diversification and the Relative Value

Investors sometimes find asset returns to be misleading, including veteran investors. As such, it is advisable to interpret asset returns in relation to the specific asset class performance. The interpretation should also take into consideration the risks that this asset class is exposed to and even the underlying currency.

When diversifying investments, it is important to think about diversifying into asset classes that come with different risk profiles. These should also be held in a variety of currencies. You should not expect to enjoy the same outcomes when investing in government bonds and technology stocks. However, it is recommended to endeavor to understand how each suits the larger investment objective.

Using such an approach, it will be possible to benefit more from a small gain from an asset within a market where the currency is increasing in value. This is as compared to a large gain from an asset within a market where the currency is in decline. As such, huge gains can translate into losses when the gains are reverted back to the stronger currency. This is the reason why it is advisable to ensure that proper research and evaluation of different asset classes are conducted.

Currencies should be considered

Currency considerations are crucial when selecting asset classes to diversify in. take the Swiss franc for instance. It is one of the world's most stable currencies and has been that way since the 1940s. Because of this reason, this particular currency can be safely and reliably used to measure the performance of other currencies.

However, private investors sometimes take too long choosing and trading stocks. Such activities are both overwhelming and time-consuming. This is why, in such instances, it is advisable to approach this differently and focus more on the asset class. With this kind of approach, it is possible to be even more profitable. Proper asset allocation is crucial to successful investing. It enables investors to mitigate any investment risks as well as portfolio volatility. The reason is that different asset classes have different reactions to all the different market conditions.

Constructing a well-thought out and aptly diversified portfolio, it is possible to have a stable and profitable portfolio that even outperforms the index of assets. Investors also have the opportunity to leverage against any potential risks because of different reactions by the different market conditions.

An Example

An investor has a total of $100,000 to invest. The best approach is to put the funds in a diversified portfolio, but the challenge is properly or adequately balancing the portfolio. The first step is to check out market conditions and then conduct an assessment of possible returns versus any likely risks. As such, the investor can choose to invest in very secure investments that are likely to produce long-term income.

Such an investment can include between 10 and 12 stocks that are highly diversified. These are generally stocks from different sectors, industries, and countries. This kind of diversification helps to leverage against any possible risks and also ensures the portfolio is thoroughly mixed.

Portfolio Diversification Approach

Disciplined Investing is a Must

Everyone is in agreement that diversification is basically the right approach. However, as an investor, there is a need to be disciplined even as you invest and diversify your investments. Investing is an art form. Put your money in equities but not all your money. Instead, think of yourself as a mutual fund manager then come up with a list of companies to invest in. You can also invest in funds and trusts like REITs or real estate investment trusts and exchange-traded funds. It is also advisable to go beyond local borders and invest globally. This way, you spread your risk around and stand chances of enjoying much better returns.

Consider Investing in Bonds and Index Funds

Apart from investing in stocks across numerous sectors, a trader may also want to invest your funds in certain fixed-income or index funds. When you invest in securities that closely keep an eye on a major index is highly recommended as you will be able to monitor progress and known when to make adjustments and so on. Such funds charge very low fees, and you will be able to easily track your investments.

Portfolio Building is a Continuous Process

Try to always grow your investments. If you receive some cash from somewhere, you can consider investing part or the entire amount into your investment portfolio. Also, keep adding regular amounts to your portfolio. You can, for instance, add about $500 each month to this portfolio to grow it at a much faster pace.

Learn the Best Exit Times

Sometimes we tend to get comfortable with the purchase-and-hold approach. This is true, especially when our investments are on autopilot. Yet a smart investor you need to keep looking out for events and special moments. Always remain abreast of events and be ready to act depending on the nature of the event. This way, you will be prepared for the moment when you have to cut your losses and exit your trades.

Watch Out for Commissions

As a trader, you need to remember that there are commissions to be paid as well as fees and charges. These charges can add up over time and become a significant amount. Therefore, keep a lookout for the charges and ensure that they are always maintained at manageable levels. In general, investing should be informative, fun, rewarding, and educational.

However, you need to be disciplined as a trader in order to be profitable in the long term and possibly outperform some of the major indices. Apart from the buy-and-hold strategy, you should diversify your portfolio, keep growing your portfolio, and learn to read the signs and know when the time is right to exit a trade. This way, your trading ventures will become extremely fruitful in the long run.

Diversification Summary

Diversification can easily be summed up using a single phrase. Never put all your eggs in one basket. This is as simple as it gets. However, the statement does not explain exactly how to go about diversification.

The idea behind portfolio diversification is simple. A trader needs to diversify into a whole group of securities, and these should be from different asset classes. It would be wrong for a portfolio to contain only stocks from one company only. Should anything happen to that company, then the investor or even trader stands to suffer huge losses, and such losses can end the investment or trade dreams of a trader.

When an investment is split into two or more different companies and asset classes, then the potential risk facing a certain product is drastically reduced. Apart from investing in more than one company, it is also a great idea to put funds in other securities such as bonds, futures, and currencies.

Traders need to develop an asset allocation strategy. Such a strategy should mostly focus on investment in stocks and bonds. Asset allocation is closely related to diversification because when done properly, asset allocation leads to a sustainably diversified portfolio.

There are other additions that can secure a portfolio and improve its diversification. These include mutual funds that consist of varied securities. A mutual fund is generally a diversified investment so diversifying into a fund helps in further diversification of a portfolio.

It is advisable to learn how to arrive at a desirable risk to reward ratio. Such a ratio can help determine the best way to diversify funds. A risk-reward ratio provides the opportunity to enjoy a particular rate of return for those willing to assume a small level of risk. Therefore, those willing to take on higher risk levels are more likely to benefit more compared to those assuming lower levels of risk.

There are some who prefer lower risk levels because perhaps of their limited resources or perhaps they prefer minimal complications. Such investors simply mirror a single and balanced fund. Others choose to simply invest in the fund. However, this can be viewed as simplistic by others who may wish for a more diversified approach.

In conclusion, diversification is key for sustainable investment, especially in the long run. It is not just more profitable but provides a risk management element into the entire investment portfolio process. Finding a suitable balance in the choice of assets provides a great approach to apt diversification.

Reducing Day Trading Risks

Risk Management

With any trade, risk management is an essential component despite the fact that it is often overlooked. It is crucial that day; traders learn about risk management if they are to successfully trade and remain profitable in the long term. The good news is that there are some simple strategies that can be adopted to ensure that trades are protected and risks management appropriately.

Basically, risk management is one of the most important aspects of the life of any serious day trader.

The reason is that a trader can actually see 90% of their trades make money, but the 10% losing money may result in a net loss if there is no proper risk management. Therefore, it is important to plan all trades carefully and to take measures to protect all trades against any losses.

Trades should be Planned Appropriately

It is a well-known fact that a good strategy will win the war rather than the battle. A good day trader needs to plan and come up with a winning strategy as the first step. A lot of traders often live by the mantra, "Plan the trade and trade the plan." This is also very similar to war planning because those who plan properly are likely to win.

Take Profit and Stop Loss Points

Traders need to come up with two very important points. These points represent two major keys that enable traders to plan ahead or in advance. A good day trader ideally knows their entry point as well as their exit points. These important points will guide the trades and will indicate at what point the trader should buy stocks and at what point the stocks should be sold off.

When a trader determines the price they wish to pay for a stock and the price they wish to sell, then it is possible to find out the likelihood of the stock performing as desired. If this can be measured and confirmed, then the trader should enter and execute the trade.

Also, traders who enter a trade without making these kinds of determinations are likely to suffer loss and will in effect cease trading and instead gamble with his resources. Whenever traders start to make losses, they believe that they can always recover their money if they invest more. This is often a lack of discipline, and the trader is likely to lose even more money.

A stop-loss is defined as the actual price where a trader will choose to sell a stock and incur a loss on the particular trade. This is a situation that happens when trades do not proceed according to the trader's plans. These points are ideally designed in order to limit losses before they get out of hand. It is always tempting for a trader who is losing money to hang in there in the hope that the losing trend will end and profitability will resume once again.

Converse to this is the take-profit point. It is important to set the take-profit, which is really the price at which a trader exits a trade by selling the security and then takes a profit from the sale. The take point is often the point at which any additional upside will become limited beyond this point. Let us assume the trade approaches a key resistance level after a large upward movement then traders can choose to exit the trade at this point.

Improving the Risk Management Process

1. Setting the Risk: Reward Ratio

When an entry signal is sighted, work out the most appropriate place to locate the stop loss than first take the profit order. As soon as a suitable price level for the orders is noted, the next step is to determine the risk versus reward ratio. Now should the outcome not be satisfactory, then it is advisable to quit the trade. Traders should generally not attempt to reduce the stop loss or widen the profit order. Discipline, at this point, is very important.

Rewards in trade are never certain and are the only potential. It is the risk that traders have control over so it should be seriously considered. A lot of the time, inexperienced traders will take the opposite approach and later suffer the consequences.

2. Traders should Avoid Break-even Stops

Creating a no-risk trade by locating the stop loss close to the entry point is something that should be avoided at all costs. The reason is that this is a dangerous move and most often not profitable. While seeking some protection is advisable, these kinds of moves cause more harm than good and should always be avoided.

3. Fixed Stop Distances should not be used

Sometimes a trader may wish to make use of a fixed number of points on the stop loss then place profit orders on markets and varied instruments. These are essentially shortcuts and should not be used under any circumstances. The reason is that they often neglect price movements and the general operation of the markets.

Also, things such as momentum and volatility are never static but always changing depending on various factors. These will also have an effect on the price movement and will affect fluctuations over time. When volatility is high, profit order points and stop loss points need to be wider to maximize profits during price swings and to prevent any premature stop runs.

4. Risk-Reward and Win-Rate Ratios should be compared together

There are traders who do not believe in the win-rate ratio and consider it irrelevant. This is actually not a wise thought because it is a very important metric. Win-rate on its own is not a very useful metric, but when pitted against the risk vs. reward ratio, then it provides important insights.

Traders should Work Out their expected Returns

Traders need to be able to work out any expected returns from their trades. Now both take-profit and stop-loss points are essential to work out this figure. Expected returns provide an important figure that cannot be underestimated. This figure that results from the calculations causes a trader to think and rationalize their trades. It also ensures that only the most profitable trades are chosen.

How to Set the Stop-Loss Points

It is the technical analysis that mostly helps to determine the take-profit and stop-loss points. However, fundamental analysis of the stocks in question does play a crucial role, especially with the timing. For instance, if a trader is holding stock and the earnings report is around the corner, then such a trader will have to dispose of those shares before the news affects the markets. This is necessary regardless of whether the stock has hit the profit margin or not.

One of the most popular ways of setting up these points is to use the well-known Moving Average. Moving averages are pretty simple to work out and are tracked closely by market players. Some of the important Moving Averages include the 9, 20, 50, 100, and 200-day averages. These should typically be applied to any stock in question and then making a determination as to whether they have had an effect on its price or not.

Also, the support and resistance trend lines can be used to place the take-profit and stop-loss levels. First, the trader needs to draw these lines simply by connecting all the past lows or highs that appeared on the above average and significant volumes. The main aim here is to effectively determine the levels where the stock price is affected by the trend lines when volumes are significantly high.

Traders need to be able to determine at what points they enter and exit any traders that they wish to participate in. This determination needs to be made before the trade is actually entered. When indicators such as the stop-loss are effectively used, then the trader will be able to minimize their losses and also reduce the frequency with which trades are excited unnecessarily. The bottom line here is to prepare early, well ahead of time so as to be sure of success in all trades.

Chapter 12 Managing Risk in Trading and the Role of Journaling

The first thing you need to know as a trader is that you will run volumes of trades and experience a lot of risks. Trading the markets is one of the riskiest investment techniques, and many people go for day trading because they have the potential for higher gains over a short period. If you have a small account, day trading gives you the chance to grow small accounts in such a short timeframe.

Risk comes about because you have to execute hundreds of trades in such a short time. You also have the capacity to place any trade you want, for as low as $500 or as high as $25,000 in a single trade. The trades are also at high speed, which means the market can swing any way – up or down. The direction of the market determines whether you make a loss or a profit.

Day trading gives you two realms of strategies to go with – high risk trading strategies or Lowe risk strategies. The goal of a successful trader is to maximize profit while lowering risks. Every time you place a trade, you need to evaluate the risk of the trade and then weight it against the potential reward. Often times this is made worse by our emotional reaction to various price directions. For instance, since you experienced a loss recently, the next logical step would be to take a higher risk on the next trade so that you can compensate on the loss. Experienced traders have a heightened level of awareness that they use to recognize a loss and reward and will make sure they take the right decision. However, you have to learn the skill over time.

You can develop a sense of decision making by keeping a journal as you trade and then reviewing the notes after the close of the market.

Different Types of risk

When talking about risk, you need to consider the different types in order for you to understand what we are saying. As a day trader, your primary role is to know the distance between the entry and the stop. Stop loss needs to be based on a resistance area on the chart or recent support.

Majority of your losses need to happen when a trade hits the stop price. This means you won't make any profit on whatever you are trading.

The second type of risk id the volatility of the market. As day traders, volatility is a friend to all of us, but it is also risky because markets that are extremely volatile tend to result in higher losses than what you actually planned for. Since there is a sense of inherent risk in trading, you need to try and avoid placing a trade when the volatility cannot be predicted, for instance when there is breaking news.

The other type of risk is exposure risk. Exposure results when you multiply the price of shares by the number of held shares. As an investor, you increase this risk when you hold on positions for a very long time. To mitigate this risk, you need to hold onto shares for a short time.

If you are holding onto large positions for a long time you stand to experience stock halts. Halts can take hours or days, though they are rare. The most common halts are those waiting for the release of news or volatility halts. Anytime a stock halts, it can lead to a different price. The biggest risk is that the stock might reopen at a very different price, which might be lower than the current price of the stock. You can take steps to reduce the effect of the halts by understanding what leads to the halts in the first place.

Journaling

If you are looking at a routine that is easy to implement and that can change the way you trade, then think about keeping a journal. The journal is a little black book that details what you do each day.

The aim of keeping a journal is to help improve your setups so that you use your experiences to analyze and help refine your trading while you improve the whole experience.

Here, we look at all you need to come up with a journal and maintain it.

What is A Journal?

A trading journal is a way to keep track of what you are doing o daily basis as a day trader. You jot down notes of what you do each day especially the different trades (or lack of) and the results of any action you take.

The trading journal needs to be tailored to your trading styles and preferences. You can keep the journal in a physical notebook or a detailed digital document on your computer. Regardless of the format, when maintained with due diligence, the trading journal can be the best way to make you a better day trader.

How Does the Trading Journal Help You Achieve Better Trades?

There are a number of ways in which a trading journal will help you become better at what you do.

Many traders attribute their success to creating and maintaining a trading journal. By noting down the different trades, you are able to check the progress over time. This allows you to find out what is working or not and change or modify them to succeed.

Helps You develop discipline in Trading

Having a trading journal helps you develop discipline as you trade. How does it do so? Well, it forces you to follow the guidelines that you have set down.

The sense of accountability that you get when you have a trading journal makes sure you are responsible for research and trading. If you know what you need to keep a log each day, you do it without fail. Making sure you log your trades and whatever happens requires a lot of discipline. Good habits such as these require you to go straight when executing trades.

Helps You Master Your Emotions

One of the top suggestions to help you run trades the right way is to trade like you are not human. Machines do not have emotions and approach all the processes in a scientific way.

However, this is easier said than done. When you get in a position to lose money, usually you find it tough getting emotion out of the way.

Keeping a journal can help you keep the emotions out of the way. With a journal in place, you get to keep track of how you feel emotionally in various trading stages. This is just to keep the emotions in check.

With time, you realize that there is a pattern that is emerging, for instance, you might find yourself getting calmer and taking orders the right way each time.

Improves Your Risk Management Practices

Day trading comes with a high level of risk. This is something that you cannot change at all because it is the nature of the market for things to run this way. However, there are various ways in which you can mitigate these risks. For one, you need to invest a large amount of research and study to give you the knowledge that you need to choose the least risky trades possible.

With a journal, you can learn things about risk tolerance. For instance, you might find that you have consistently been able to hold positions for longer and you have been losing profits as a result. You might also find that you have issues getting out of trades because you have been taking positions that are too big for your stage.

By looking at the risks that you have been taking and how they affect the results you return, you get to make adjustments.

For instance, you might exit trades sooner or you might end up taking smaller positions based on the results you return. This way you help reduce risks and improve risk management.

Creating the Perfect Trading Diary

Now that you know how effective the trading journal is, you need to know how to come up with the best one. Here are a few tips for success when coming up with a journal:

- Be consistent

Trading needs you to have a routine. You will probably get the most out of the journal if you have a routine that you follow religiously.

You also need to follow the routine to the latter. This means that you are consistent with what you do day in day out. For instance, you need to wake up early each day to prepare for trading. This allows you to get errands and tasks out of the way early and gives you to do research so that you are ready to roll when the market starts.

This is a directive though because since many traders are doing other responsibilities, you need to come up with the right schedule that works for you. Choose the routine that will work for you and that you can stick to easily.

- Analyze the Market

The more the trades that you track, the more data you have to deal with and the more you get to learn and the faster you do it.

By recording the trades, overall thoughts, market observations and more, you aren't just learning from the mistakes that you are doing, but you are also gaining a sense of how to perform the right market analysis.

For instance, with the right trading data, you get to notice gains and losses in a particular industry or sector. This can give you clues on the trends in the market that you might have missed out.

Once you see what is working and what isn't, you get to have a targeted market analysis.

- Analyze and Come Up with Your Own Setups

A trading journal allows you to come up with the right setups. Here is how this works out:

- Find the setups that trigger trade entry

When do you enter the market? The trading journal helps you figure everything out. You need to go into each trade with a plan. However, if you realize that you are entering trades too soon or too late based on the journal, you can then decide to try something different.

With the perfect trading journal, you have the capacity to determine the setups that trigger the entries.

- Gain Insight into the Market

When you record your own setups, you have the ability to gain insight into the market that you are trading in. you get to notice market trends and how they might end up affecting the setups.

As a trader, understanding the way the market runs is ideal because it helps you to keep up to date. The market is dynamic, and the setups that work in one market condition might not work for other conditions. When you understand the market, you get to navigate around and acclimatize to new markets.

- Know the Appropriate Lot Size

In any market, the lot size means the number of shares which you buy in any transaction. The theory of size allows you to regulate price quotes. It is basically the size of the trade that you place in the financial market.

With price regulation being a part of every market, you need to always be aware of the number of units that you purchase eon contract, and determine the price you pay per unit.

Make sure you keep track of the lot sizes that you deal with in any trade, as it helps you to decide the types of approaches that you take in the future.

- Determine the Style of Trading

Many traders choose to be one type of trader or another. Many of them do it by force, which is a fact that isn't the best. As a trader, you need to naturally gravitate towards a specific trading style, and not force it.

Rather than chasing after what is trendy or what you have seen other traders do, it is advisable to focus on a style of trading that gives you profit, whether you go after long or short positions.

A trading journal can help you determine the type of trade that is best suited for you by giving you a summary of the trades that gave you money.

- Understand Profit Placement

Trading is a probability game, with so many moving pieces that make it work. With so many parts that are needed to make everything work, you need to make sure you get everything right the first time. This isn't easy at all.

Here are a few specifics that you need to master:

- *Cut losses fast*: you need to learn to cut losses quickly, which means you pull out of a position earlier than later, even if it means missing out on a few profits. It is always good to be safe than sorry. Having a trading journal helps you determine when to get out of a trade. If you notice that you are losing constantly, then journaling can help you learn how to cut losses fast. Additionally, if you notice that you are getting out of trades too early, then you can start staying gin the game a little bit longer.

- *Stop losses*: you need to learn how to come up with the best stop loss order. The order can help you release the order when you reach a particular price. With the right stop loss order, you can buy the security rather than selling it when you reach a certain price. Make sure you record the different entry and exit positions; how much you have risked and the results of everything. As the information collects over time, you can determine what your best setups are so that you can focus on replicating the profits you gained in the past to eliminate losses.

Apart from this information, you also need to record other things so that you make the most out of each entry:

- *The date*: this shouldn't be left out of the journal. Not only does it help you to track what you were doing and when you were doing it, but it allows you to go back and look at the performance of the stock on that date in future. Never assume that you will rack everything in your brain!

- *The Time Frame*: do not just record the date, but make sure you know the perfect time for each entry. In the world of trading, minutes matter. Trading in the morning can make a huge difference compared to trading in the afternoon. For instance, the setup that works for you during the morning hours might not work the same way in the afternoon.
- *Price in*: this is the point where the journal starts working well with the trading plan. When coming up with a trading plan, you set the key tactics such as the entry point, the exit and what you plan to gain from this trade. This helps you to stick to the plan and then keep emotions out of things. In the journal, make sure you note the price at which you entered a successful trade.
- *Price out*: don't just mark the time that you entered the trade – also take note of the price that you exit the trade too. The exit is also as vital as the entrance. Keeping this data allows you to analyze whether you are staying in a position for the right amount of time. Note any difficulties that you encounter getting out of

the position, as this might affect the level of risk next time.

- *Amount you are risking*: before you enter a trade, you need to determine the amount of money you plan to put into the trade. Note: The money you put tin should be an amount you can risk losing. So, how much money should you risk on a trade? The answer is that you need to always take a cautious position, and never try to risk what you can't lose. You do not want to enter into a trade and blow up the account as this might trigger emotional trading.

Tips for Creating an Efficient Trading Journal

1. Identify the Patterns That lead to Losses

As a trader, you can't eliminate the risk of making losses. For many traders, the success rate is 70 percent, and many of them know that the 100 percent win rate is a myth.

You can never control how much you win, but you can at least control the amount you can lose by cutting losses fast.

You also get to learn from the losses. Once you have a trading journal, you begin to identify patterns that lead to losses and assess what is happening.

2. Identify the Patterns That Have Made You Profit

As a trader, you not only focus on the things that went wrong, but also look at what went right as well. You need to chart patterns in the trades to help you analyze what make you the most money. Many successful traders base their success on being able to identify patterns. Many depend on stock charts, but later realize that even the trading journal gives them an insight into what they need to do.

3. Go for Professional Assistance

Trading classes give you an asset that you will never regret in your trading life. Even with the right data, you might find yourself failing to make profitable trades because you do not have the mechanics to make things work for you. When you take time to learn the mechanics of trading, you find that you have the basis to identify key indicators and add them to the journal.

Just like any other trade, the more you get prepared to execute trades the more successful you become. The knowledge originates from previous traders that have become successful in their efforts.

4. Work With templates

Templates make it easy for you to come up with a plan. There are many platforms online that offer you both paid and free templates that you can use to create the perfect journal, all you need to do is to choose the one that suits you then customize it to your liking. As you become more adept, you find that the journal becomes your best friend, and it also becomes more detailed.

Chapter 13 Tips and Tricks to Make Your Life Easier when Using the MT4 Platform

So far ,we've covered plenty of tips in this book. The idea is to learn them ahead of time, before working intensively with the platform, so you can increase your productivity.

SPEAKING OF PRODUCTIVITY, A QUESTION: WHAT IS THE QUICKEST WAY TO INCREASE PRODUCTIVITY WHEN THE EVERYDAY WORKING TOOL IS A COMPUTER STATION? ANSWER: REDUCE THE NUMBER OF REQUIRED CLICKS.

IF THE SAME JOB CAN BE DONE WITH HALF THE CLICKS, THAT'S A FIFTY-PERCENT TIME SAVING. SO, HERE'S OUR NEXT TIP: THE MT4 HAS AN OPTION TO REDUCE THE NUMBER OF CLICKS REQUIRED TO SELECT OBJECTS ON A CHART.

Go to Tools/Options/Objects, and make sure you check the box that says, "Select object by single mouse click".

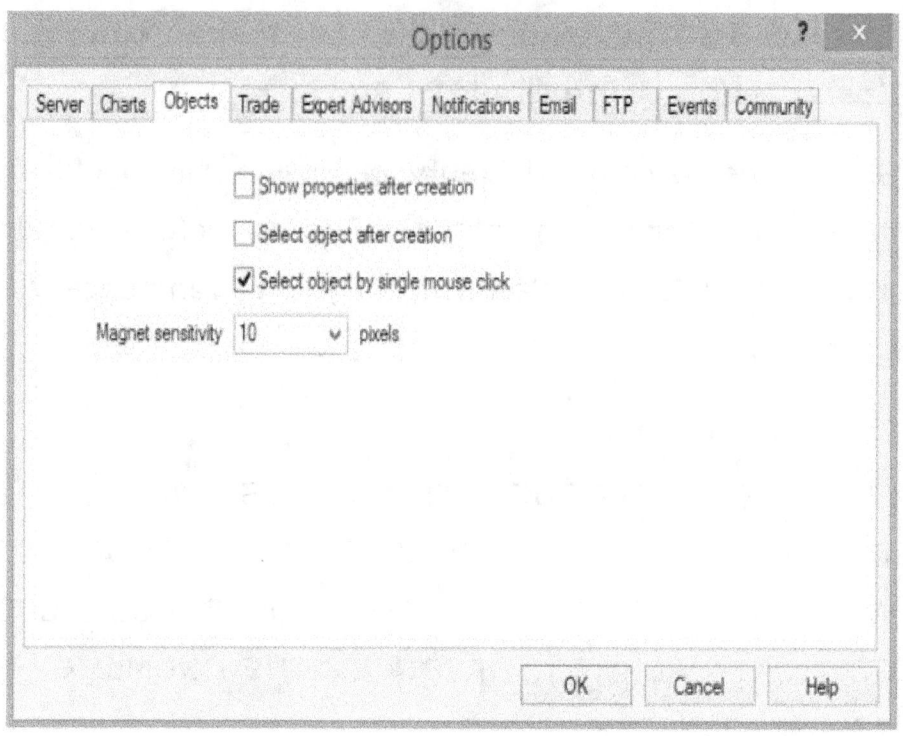

This way, when drawing a trend line, channel, or just counting waves to apply the Elliott Waves Theory, one click is enough to select the object.

Speaking of trend lines... they can use some attention too. The default setting for a trend line has it projecting it indefinitely to the right side of the screen; you'll find that annoying, not to say useless.

Solving this issue is easy. First select a trend line and right-click on it.

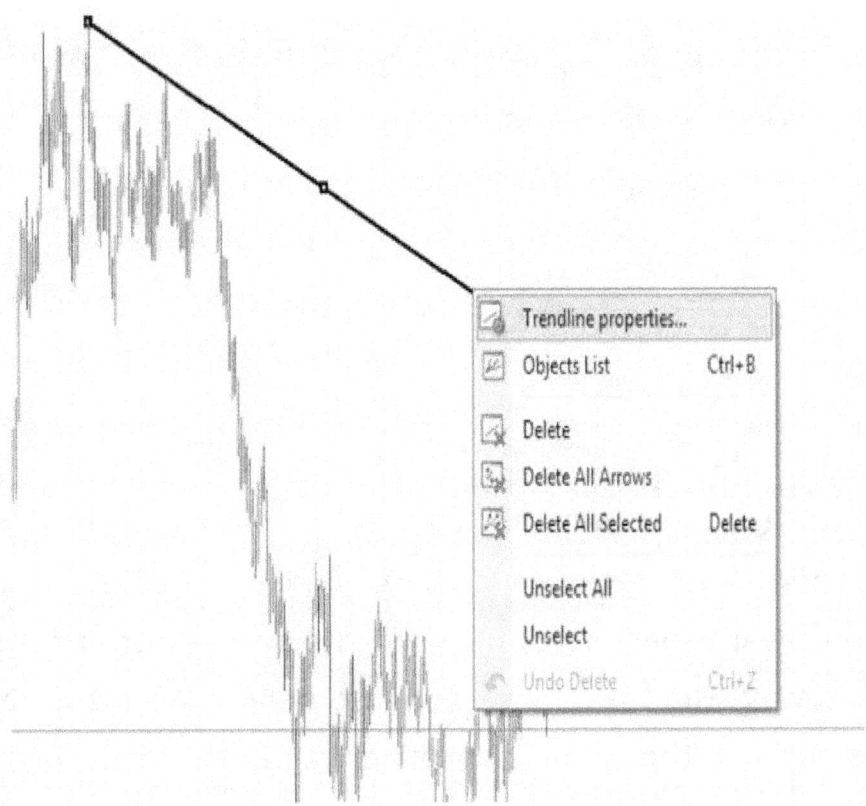

From the popup menu, select the first option: Trend line properties... In the Trend lines dialog box, go to the Parameters tab.

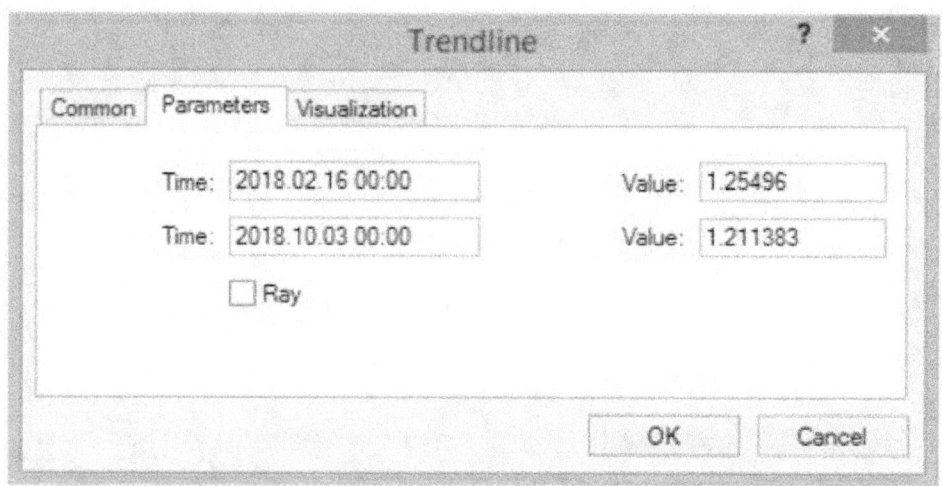

The "Ray" option is what gives the trend line the properties of a ray – i.e., extending it indefinitely. We don't want that, so make sure the box is not checked. This way, the trend line is limited only to what's drawn, or just to the time and price values entered in the dialog.

Still on the topic of trend lines and objects, another handy shortcut is to copy and paste objects. The copied object keeps the same parameters/characteristics of the original one. It's just a replica.

To copy an object, hold down the CTRL key on your keyboard and then click the object to select it. Now drag the new object to use anywhere else on the screen.

This is an essential step for all kinds of strategies. For example, when building a channel from a simple trend line, one needs to keep the angle of the second line exactly the same as the first. So, copy/paste works best.

Moreover, some traders use various colors for different trend lines coming from higher or lower timeframes. Or, as is in the case of top/down analyses with the Elliott Waves Theory, traders use color codes to illustrate various cycles within the theory.

No matter the strategy, the copy/paste function for objects is a time-saving tool you'll love when using the MT4 platform.

Another useful tip when using the MT4 is to save your work. There's nothing more frustrating than working all day on an Elliott count or strategy, making notes on charts and so on, and losing all your work. How is that possible?

Power failures, for instance, do happen. If you work on a desktop station, the MT4 will shut down in an instant, and your work won't be saved.

The MT4 only saves work on normal closing. So, if your strategy is labor-intensive, make sure to restart the MT4 platform from time to time so that the work done remains there for further use.

Conclusion

One of the most important things that you should always remember as you engage in day trading is the notion of developing a trading strategy. Never fall for the myth that your trading strategy will not work. In fact, the best forms of online trading strategies are those that work for you. Don't settle for a strategy simply because your trading partner claimed that it worked for them. Build your strategy from scratch. Test it and find a way of constantly improving it. A strategy which has been proven and tested over time will guarantee that you maximize on getting profits while reducing your risks considerably.

On the issue of risks, another essential thing to remember is having a risk management strategy. It is not surprising to learn that a trader with a 50% success rate could perform better than one with a 75% success rate. If the latter fails to use a risk mitigation strategy, then they could incur huge losses in spite of their profits. So, as part of mitigating your risks, first, know the importance of planning your trade. Without a trading plan, you will be setting yourself to fail. Equally, if you are trading using larger accounts, remember to stick to the one percent rule. Don't be greedy. Yes, the markets might seem appealing, but there is no guarantee you will continue making profits if the trend is maintained. In line with this, to help you mitigate losses and lock in profits, you should make good use of taking profit and stop loss points. The best traders in the market are using these tools. Therefore, you are not an exception.

Now, with the numerous guides and online tutorials on day trading, one will wonder why most traders fail. Surprisingly, people fail not because they lack capital but because of their mistakes. For instance, a new trader might enter the market without any plan. If the first few traders are successful, they will gain the impression that they don't need a plan to trade. The moment things turn sour, they abandon their randomness and look for other trading strategies. At the end of the day, they will be doing something else which is not trading. They will be gambling. It is important for a new trader to know of the common reasons why most traders fail. This guarantees that they know how to avoid making similar mistakes. Take, for example, the notion where new traders simply begin trading without any formal knowledge about the industry. You need to do your homework before starting to trade. Find out what other traders do on a regular basis to make sure that they close the day with profits.

When trading using a small account, you should not be discouraged by the fact that you have limited funds in your account. Indeed, managing a small account has its challenges including the fact that you will be working under pressure not to make any losses. However, you should look at the bright side. Acknowledge the fact that you are getting something out of the trading activity. Trading in a small account gives you the advantage of learning how to trade with minimal risks. As a new trader, it is imperative to embrace the importance of starting small. With time, the knowledge and experience you get will make a huge difference.

The good news is that there are proven and tested strategies which you could use to improve the small account. For instance, you could choose to risk more for every trade you buy. Also, you should always ensure that more capital is at work. Forget about securing your account. This will take away a bigger portion of the money which should have been used to trade. The idea of swinging big when there is a perfect setup to trade should be at your fingertips. Doing this warrants that you take advantage of a trading opportunity which could increase your capital. Also, you might want to forget about using stops. Using stops might hinder you from making the best out of a trade which would have performed well later on.

You will need a sober mind to succeed in day trading. Unfortunately, there are common mental errors which could affect how well you perform in your trading activity. For instance, if you lack confidence in your plan, how do you expect to stick to it? You have to believe that your plan will lead you to make profits that you anticipate. This mentality will develop a positive attitude about the whole trading activity. Therefore, you will have all the reasons to be disciplined and stick to your plans no matter the circumstances.

If you are going to trade when your mind has deviated, then there are high chances that you will fail. You need to have a clear mind free from any distractions. If you have personal issues you need to attend to, ensure that you sort them out first. Any small mistakes in day trading could cost you a lot of money. Hence, you need to be focused at all times. Still, if you are not feeling well, just stop trading. Markets are there to stay. Therefore, if you don't trade today, you can still trade tomorrow. The point here is that you need to be healthy enough to give your mind the energy it needs to make sound decisions.

Whether you are trading using a small or a large account, discipline is the key to success. If you can't stick to your strategy, it is better to try something else. Most traders have failed in day trading because of their lack of discipline. It is by being disciplined that you will know when to enter and exit the market. With discipline, you will also understand the importance of using only one percent of your trading capital.

Good luck trading!

www.ingramcontent.com/pod-product-compliance
Lightning Source LLC
Chambersburg PA
CBHW032123250526
R18348000001B/R183480PG45466CBX00046B/11